GLENCOE

VOCABULARY BUILDER

Peter Fischer, Editorial Consultant

National-Louis University

Course 6

 **Glencoe**

New York, New York   Columbus, Ohio   Chicago, Illinois   Peoria, Illinois   Woodland Hills, California

Acknowledgments

The pronunciation key used in the glossary has been reproduced by permission
from *The American Heritage Dictionary of the English Language, Fourth Edition.*
Copyright © 2000 by Houghton Mifflin Company.

 **Glencoe**

The *McGraw·Hill* Companies

Printed in the United States of America

Send all inquiries to:
Glencoe/McGraw-Hill
8787 Orion Place
Columbus, OH 43240

SE ISBN: 0-07-861670-0
ATE ISBN: 0-07-861671-9

1 2 3 4 5 6 7 8 9 10 113 10 09 08 07 06 05 04

Contents

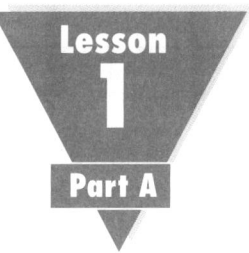

Name _____

Cuna Creations

Of the hundreds of San Blas islands that dot the Caribbean coast of Panama, only fifty are inhabited, primarily by the Cuna people. The chief claim to fame of the **denizens** of these islands lies with the women; travelogues, leisure magazines, and movies often feature their dazzling,
5 **exotic** beauty, complete with nose rings and beaded ankles and wrists. If the Cuna women are their society's ambassadors to the world, then the mola cloths that they create and wear are their flags.

Molas are vibrantly colored, intricately patterned, hand-stitched cloth panels. Cuna women, who learn the complex process from their moth-
10 ers, first stack anywhere from two to seven layers of different-colored cloth. Then they cut designs into the top layer and sew the designs' edges with **complementary** stitchery. Smaller, similar designs are cut into the succeeding layers, exposing each level of color. The final panels are often so thick that they resemble sculptural forms.

15 The **paramount** theme represented in mola design is nature. The earliest examples were abstract interpretations of the texture of brain coral, but the designs have become increasingly complex, **stylized** images of animals and plants. Although folk-art experts have attempted to **invest** the patterns with religious symbolism, the designs are probably purely decora-
20 tive. Each mola is unique; even when a motif is repeated, the final panel, blouse, purse, or pillow shows differences in color and form.

While they may appear ancient in concept, molas actually emerged in the latter half of the nineteenth century. Until missionaries and traders visited the San Blas islands, Cuna women had painted their bodies. In order to
25 conform to visitors' expectations, they transferred the bright designs to the machine-manufactured cloth that the traders brought and entered the modern world wearing molas. The word itself actually means "cloth."

The evolution of the mola **exemplifies** a necessary **dichotomy** for the Cuna—adopting new ways to survive in the modern world while at the
30 same time keeping their culture intact. The Cuna women initially made their molas for **pragmatic** reasons, without a thought to selling them. However, when traders offered to buy them, the women gladly accepted the money, returning to sewing and abandoning other duties that they had previously shared with the men. Today, the women's cottage indus-
35 try brings substantial income into an economy formerly based on coconuts and helps pay for schools, water systems, and electrical generators.

This dramatic, colorful needlework is found nowhere else in the world, and it is unlikely that **replicas** will ever be successfully made by machine. While molas are widely sought as works of art, they remain essential to the
40 Cuna women's traditional dress and their way of life.

Words

complementary

denizen

dichotomy

exemplify

exotic

invest

paramount

pragmatic

replica

stylized

Each word in this lesson's word list appears in dark type in the selection you just read. Think about how the vocabulary word is used in the selection, then write the letter for the best answer to each question.

1. *Denizens* (line 3) can best be explained as _____.
   (A) remnants   (B) inhabitants
   (C) public buildings   (D) mythological gods

   1. _____

2. Which word or words could best replace *exotic* in line 5?
   (A) made up of distinct   (B) exhausted
       elements
   (C) devoid of emotion   (D) intriguingly different

   2. _____

3. Something that is *complementary* (line 12) can best be explained as _____.
   (A) serving to complete   (B) unattractive
   (C) confusing   (D) useless

   3. _____

4. Which words could best replace *paramount* in line 15?
   (A) freed from an obligation   (B) passing away quickly
   (C) chief or major   (D) showing little preparation

   4. _____

5. Which words could best replace *stylized* in line 17?
   (A) represented in a way that   (B) causing or showing joy
       does not reflect nature
   (C) stubbornly and recklessly   (D) arousing strong dislike
       willful

   5. _____

6. Which words could best replace *invest* in line 18?
   (A) act as a go-between   (B) endow with a quality
   (C) remove extraneous matter   (D) come quickly into view
       from

   6. _____

7. Which words could best replace *exemplifies* in line 28?
   (A) displays in order to impress   (B) persists in a state of inactivity
       others
   (C) relies on for support   (D) illustrates by example

   7. _____

8. A *dichotomy* (line 28) can best be explained as _____.
   (A) two conflicting parts or   (B) a tradition passed down through
       opinions   the generations
   (C) two or more figures that   (D) one of three major divisions
       make up a unit or design

   8. _____

9. Which word could best replace *pragmatic* in line 31?
   (A) interdependent   (B) charitable
   (C) practical   (D) damaging

   9. _____

10. *Replicas* (line 38) can best be explained as _____.
    (A) openings in fabric   (B) earnest requests
    (C) multiple shadows   (D) copies or reproductions of originals

    10. _____

Applying Meaning

Decide which word in parentheses best completes the sentence. Then write
the sentence, adding the missing word.

1. The woman wore a small _____ of an ancient statue on a thick chain
   around her neck. (denizen; replica)

   _____

   _____

   _____

2. In his autobiography, Benjamin Franklin offered _____ advice for
   achieving success. (complementary; pragmatic)

   _____

   _____

   _____

3. The coelacanth (sē′lə-kănth′), originally thought to be extinct, was
   discovered by scientists to be one of the _____ of extraordinarily deep
   ocean water. (denizens; dichotomies)

   _____

   _____

   _____

4. Once regarded as _____ and difficult to grow, orchids have become
   common houseplants. (exotic; stylized)

   _____

   _____

   _____

5. Because of his enormous size and ugliness, people have unfairly _____
   Dr. Frankenstein's monster with evil, when the poor creature was actually lonely and afraid. (exemplified; invested)

   _____

   _____

   _____

Read each sentence below. Write "correct" on the answer line if the vocabulary word has been used correctly. Write "incorrect" on the answer line if the vocabulary word has been used incorrectly.

6. The chance to play at world-famous Carnegie Hall is of *paramount* importance to many musicians.

6. _____

7. The encyclopedia article, along with the *complementary* information in the magazine, enabled Flora to write the research paper.

7. _____

8. The logo of the publishing company was a stylized owl.

8. _____

9. A crystal, which has a rigid geometrical structure marked by symmetry, is a naturally occurring *dichotomy*.

9. _____

10. Residue from DDT, an insecticide, has been shown to *exemplify* in the ecosystem and the food chain long after its original use.

10. _____

For each word used incorrectly, write a sentence using the word properly.

_____

_____

_____

_____

_____

_____

_____

_____

Mastering Meaning

Imagine that a former student at your high school has donated several paintings, which have been hung in the cafeteria. Since you are the music and movie critic for the school newspaper, the editor has asked you to try your hand at an art review. Envision the paintings and in your review, include both their pleasing and displeasing aspects. You may look in art books or encyclopedias for examples of paintings. Use some of the words you studied in this lesson.

Name _____

Some real and fictional people and places are so memorable for their characteristics that their name has come to have new meaning. Sometimes the name has so thoroughly taken on this meaning that it is no longer capitalized. All the words in this lesson came from proper nouns.

Unlocking Meaning

Read the brief descriptions of the people and places below. Then choose the word or phrase that correctly completes the sentence. Write the letter for your choice on the answer line.

Nicolas Chauvin, a French soldier in a nineteenth-century play, was noted for his extreme patriotism and his excessive devotion to Napoleon, the emperor of France. The noun *chauvinism* has come to mean _____.

   1. (A) rebel
      (B) prejudiced belief in the superiority of one's own group
      (C) admiration for the leader of one's country
      (D) French soldier

Around 600 B.C., a Greek politician named Draco set up a system of laws in Athens. These laws were extremely unpopular among Athenians because they were so strict and so severe. The adjective *draconian* has come to mean _____.

   2. (A) illegal
      (B) ancient
      (C) political
      (D) harsh

Although Hector was the noblest Trojan in Homer's *Iliad*, in medieval drama he was often portrayed as a braggart and an intimidator. A synonym for *hector* is _____.

   3. (A) actor
      (B) dramatist
      (C) warrior
      (D) bully

In his most famous work, entitled *The Prince*, Niccolo Machiavelli suggested that rulers use whatever methods necessary to achieve and maintain power, no matter how immoral those methods might be. From his name we get the adjective *Machiavellian*, which means _____.

   4. (A) masculine
      (B) characterized by deceit and cunning
      (C) living forever
      (D) of royal blood

Words

- chauvinism
- draconian
- hector
- Machiavellian
- martinet
- saturnine
- silhouette
- stentorian
- sybarite
- tawdry

1. _____

2. _____

3. _____

4. _____

Jean Martinet, an officer in the French army in the 1600s, demanded a strict following of rules and regulations by all of his subordinates. Today the noun *martinet* means _____.

  5. (A) rigid disciplinarian

   (B) stubborn rule-breaker

   (C) French country dance

   (D) easygoing authority figure

5. _____

The planet Saturn revolves around the Sun approximately once every 29.5 years—that's more than twenty-nine times longer than it takes Earth to go the same distance. Also, because it is so far from the Sun, Saturn is much colder than Earth. A *saturnine* person is _____.

  6. (A) distant, but warm

   (B) satisfied

   (C) bright and lively

   (D) cold and sullen

6. _____

Étienne de Silhouette was an eighteenth-century French finance minister, whose drastic cuts in spending resulted in people linking his name with anything plain or cheap. Today, a *silhouette* is a _____.

  7. (A) simple, inexpensive outline portrait

   (B) farm structure for storing animal feed

   (C) financial wizard

   (D) politician

7. _____

Stentor was a Greek herald in the Trojan War. According to Homer's *Iliad,* his voice was as loud as that of fifty men combined. A synonym for *stentorian* is _____.

  8. (A) soft-spoken

   (B) ancient

   (C) extremely loud

   (D) warlike

8. _____

Sybarites were the citizens of Sybaris, an ancient city known for luxurious living. Nowadays, a *sybarite* is a person who is ____.

  9. (A) unduly serious

   (B) devoted to pleasure

   (C) extremely poor

   (D) ancient

9. _____

In 679 A.D., Saint Audrey died of a throat tumor which, according to legend, was caused by the fancy necklaces she had enjoyed wearing as a young woman. Years later, fairs held in her honor sold flashy and cheap scarves and necklaces. The pronunciation of "Saint Audrey" gradually changed to "tawdry," an adjective which means _____.

  10. (A) tastelessly showy

   (B) heavenly

   (C) sickly

   (D) elegant

10. _____

Name _____

Applying Meaning

Decide which word in parentheses best completes the sentence. Then write the sentence, adding the missing word.

1. The new principal announced a set of strict rules that were absolutely _____. (draconian; tawdry)

   _____

   _____

   _____

2. With his wild, exaggerated gestures and his _____ voice, he's extremely hard to ignore. (Machiavellian; stentorian)

   _____

   _____

   _____

3. The excessive makeup and loud clothing made the young actress look cheap and _____. (saturnine; tawdry)

   _____

   _____

   _____

4. When it comes to enforcing the community center rules, Mr. Toddino is a real _____. (martinet; sybarite)

   _____

   _____

   _____

5. The speaker showed his _____ when he answered only the men's questions after the lecture. (chauvinism; silhouette)

   _____

   _____

   _____

6. She doesn't do anything quickly or with passion; she is the most _____ person I've ever encountered. (saturnine; tawdry)

   _____

   _____

   _____

7. The highlights of President Abraham Lincoln's _____ were his angular nose and prominent chin. (martinet; silhouette)

_____

_____

_____

Match the description in Column B with the word in Column A. Write the letter of the correct answer on the line provided.

Column A	Column B	
8. Machiavellian	a. a boss who fires an employee for arriving at work two minutes late	**8.** _____
9. stentorian	b. an athlete who constantly picks on teammates	**9.** _____
10. saturnine	c. a political candidate who doesn't mind breaking a few rules to win	**10.** _____
11. hector	d. a person with the enthusiasm and energy of a slug	**11.** _____
12. martinet	e. a teacher whose loud voice gives you a headache	**12.** _____

Cultural Literacy Note

Faustian bargain

According to German legend, Johann Faust was a magician and astrologer who made an extraordinary and horrifying deal with the devil. There are several versions of this legend. In all of them, Faust agrees to sell his soul to the devil in exchange for youth, power, and knowledge. Today, if someone is said to have struck a "Faustian bargain," it suggests that the person is willing to sacrifice anything, even spiritual values, for power, knowledge, and material gain.

Cooperative Learning: Work with a partner to do additional research on the legend of Faust. Try to find and read one or more summaries of the stories and plays based on the legend. Then work together to write a description of a modern-day Faust that you have read or heard about.

Copyright © Glencoe/McGraw-Hill, a division of The McGraw-Hill Companies, Inc.

Name _____

Many familiar words have the Latin root -*spec*-, which comes from the Latin word *specere*, meaning "to look at." Another common Latin root is -*plic*-, from the Latin word *plicare*, meaning "to fold." This root appears in English words in a variety of spellings. The vocabulary words in this lesson all have one of these roots.

Root	Meaning	English Word
-spec- -spic-	to look at	speculate auspicious
-plic-	to fold	implicate

Unlocking Meaning

A vocabulary word appears in italics in each sentence or short passage below. Find the root in each vocabulary word and choose the letter for the correct definition. Write the letter for your choice on the answer line.

Under the *auspices* of the Afterschool Academic and Athletic Program, the teens in this neighborhood have developed better study and exercise habits. The helpful support of the counselors there has meant better grades and healthier bodies for my friends and me.

1. (A) discouragement
  (B) affection and trust
  (C) objection
  (D) support and guidance

Our softball season got off to an *auspicious* start, with our team winning the first three games by wide margins.

2. (A) awful; terrible
  (B) slow and cautious
  (C) marked by success
  (D) early

Ms. Trahn said that Nick's oral report on how the destruction of the rainforest threatens the fragile ecosystem of our planet was interesting and well organized. She did, however, ask him to *explicate* two terms that had not been clearly defined.

3. (A) eliminate
  (B) apply
  (C) replace
  (D) explain

Words

auspices

auspicious

explicate

implicate

introspective

perspicuity

plait

pliant

specious

speculate

1.  _____

2. _____

3. _____

The thief confessed to robbing the bank alone and did not *implicate* anyone else.

4. (A) burden

    (B) analyze the motives of

    (C) embarrass

    (D) involve or cause to appear guilty

4. _____

For years, Kendra listened politely to everyone else's ideas and opinions about what she should do with her life. Then she realized that being *introspective* was the only way she'd learn what her own thoughts were on the subject.

5. (A) tending to ignore other people's thoughts and feelings

    (B) inclined to examine one's own feelings and thoughts

    (C) showing an eagerness to discuss one's own thoughts and feelings

    (D) having a tendency to speak without thinking

5. _____

Although the topic was extremely complicated, Jeanette had no trouble understanding the article because of the *perspicuity* of the writing.

6. (A) clearness   (B) complexity

    (C) dullness   (D) repetitive nature

6. _____

Kim, playing the role of Juliet, appeared onstage wearing a white gown with a light blue overdress. Her long black hair hung in a single *plait* down her back. A blue silk ribbon had been woven through it.

7. (A) bushy mane   (B) wig

    (C) braid   (D) curl

7. _____

Some people think that I have a *pliant* nature and that they can boss me around and tell me what to do. Sometimes I am like that, but I can also be really difficult and stubborn.

8. (A) not quickly influenced   (B) easily controlled

    (C) obstinate   (D) adventurous

8. _____

The girl's *specious* argument was believable enough to convince everyone of her innocence. It was only later that we discovered her deception and lies.

9. (A) appearing true but actually false

    (B) honest

    (C) highly exaggerated

    (D) long

9. _____

I was shocked when I heard Tessa lie to Dad, since she had always lectured me about being honest. I could *speculate* about her motives forever, but unless I asked her, I would never discover why she had done it.

10. (A) wonder

    (B) whine

    (C) laugh out loud

    (D) argue vehemently

10. _____

Applying Meaning

Read each sentence or short passage below. Write "correct" on the answer line if the vocabulary word has been used correctly. Write "incorrect" on the answer line if the vocabulary word has been used incorrectly.

1. Getting a speeding ticket before we were even out of our own city was an *auspicious* way to start our vacation.

2. The writer obviously knew her topic. The *perspicuity* of her essay showed that she had a thorough and clear understanding of the subject.

3. The climber's foot became trapped between two boulders, and she could not *explicate* it without injuring it.

4. When he testified at the congressional hearing, he gave a *specious* argument about the glory of war.

5. After brushing her long golden locks, Jana began to *plait* her hair into two braids.

6. Under the *auspices* of the famine relief organization, all food supplies were cut off to the starving villagers.

1. _____

2. _____

3. _____

4. _____

5. _____

6. _____

For each word used incorrectly, write a sentence using the word properly.

_____

_____

_____

_____

_____

_____

_____

_____

_____

_____

Follow the directions below to write a sentence using a vocabulary word.

7. Describe an athlete after losing an important game. Use the word *introspective*.

_____

_____

_____

8. Tell what might happen if a criminal is caught but his partners in crime aren't. Use the word *implicate*.

_____

_____

_____

9. Describe a prize-winning director and a young, aspiring actor in his first movie. Use the word *pliant*.

_____

_____

_____

10. Tell what someone might say when asked about today's weather. Use the word *speculate*.

_____

_____

_____

Bonus Word

espionage

Someone who secretly obtains information about one government and then sells or gives that information to another government is engaging in an act of espionage. The word *espionage* comes from the Old French word *espier,* meaning "to watch."

Write a Paragraph: What do you think about someone who engages in espionage against his or her own government? Do you think governments should engage in espionage? Write a paragraph describing your thoughts on the subject.

Name _____

How well do you remember the words you studied in Lessons 1 through 3?
Take the following test covering the words from the last three lessons.

Part 1 Choose the Correct Meaning

Each question below includes a word in capital letters, followed by four words
or phrases. Choose the word or phrase that is <u>closest</u> in meaning to the word
in capital letters. Write the letter for your answer on the line provided.

Sample

S. FINISH	(A) enjoy	(B) complete	S. _____**B**_____
	(C) destroy	(D) enlarge	

1. TAWDRY	(A) tan in color	(B) cheap and gaudy	1. _____
	(C) talkative	(D) valuable	
2. SPECIOUS	(A) roomy	(B) distinctive	2. _____
	(C) risky or dangerous	(D) appealing but false	
3. DENIZEN	(A) inhabitant	(B) legal representative	3. _____
	(C) unit of weight	(D) place of worship	
4. INTROSPECTIVE	(A) spectacular	(B) concerned with manners	4. _____
	(C) thoughtful	(D) rude	
5. HECTOR	(A) ridicule	(B) criticize	5. _____
	(C) bully	(D) thoughtless	
6. PARAMOUNT	(A) of primary importance	(B) side by side	6. _____
	(C) geometric figure	(D) shortened	
7. PLAIT	(A) leafy plant	(B) flexibility	7. _____
	(C) playful	(D) braid	
8. CHAUVINISM	(A) strict religious beliefs	(B) fanatical patriotism	8. _____
	(C) love of colorful clothing	(D) type of modern art	
9. REPLICA	(A) detailed account	(B) replacement	9. _____
	(C) copy	(D) blame	

Go on to next page. ➤

10. DRACONIAN   (A) unusually strong   (B) of a dull color   **10.** _____
                                (C) honest   (D) harsh and severe

11. AUSPICIOUS   (A) highly favorable   (B) evident   **11.** _____
                                (C) suspicious   (D) tastefully presented

12. SYBARITE   (A) honored citizen   (B) person devoted to excessive luxury   **12.** _____
                                (C) valuable mineral   (D) habitual liar

13. COMPLEMENTARY   (A) flattering   (B) complicated   **13.** _____
                                (C) serving to complete   (D) made of many parts

14. EXPLICATE   (A) remove carefully   (B) confuse thoroughly   **14.** _____
                                (C) examine scientifically   (D) explain

15. MARTINET   (A) type of small bird   (B) rigid disciplinarian   **15.** _____
                                (C) lazy, unproductive worker   (D) distant relative

Part 2 Matching Words and Meanings

Match the definition in Column B with the word in Column A.
Write the letter of the correct definition on the line provided.

Column A	Column B	
16. dichotomy	a. excitingly strange	**16.** _____
17. stentorian	b. protection and support	**17.** _____
18. exemplify	c. division into two opposite parts or opinions	**18.** _____
19. auspices	d. to involve or connect closely	**19.** _____
20. perspicuity	e. serious and sullen	**20.** _____
21. speculate	f. illustrate	**21.** _____
22. saturnine	g. clearness	**22.** _____
23. exotic	h. to wonder and theorize	**23.** _____
24. pragmatic	i. extremely loud	**24.** _____
25. implicate	j. practical	**25.** _____

Name _____

The Birth of the International Red Cross

On June 25, 1859, a Swiss banker witnessed a battle and its aftermath—
an experience that would change his life and the lives of millions more.
Jean Henri Dunant was in Italy, hoping to get the authorization of
Emperor Napoleon III to import windmills into what was then the French

5 colony of Algeria. He never got his interview with Napoleon. Instead, the
emperor and his ally, the king of Sardinia, **mobilized** troops against
Austria in the hill town of Solferino. Dunant spent the days that followed
the battle working among the thousands of injured soldiers. "The gen-
tleman in white," as the soldiers called him, knelt in the dust in his linen

10 suit, bathing their **festering** wounds and offering sips of water.

On his return to Geneva, Switzerland, Dunant was **beset** with concern
over the lack of organized medical care on the battlefield. Obsessed with
the idea of trying to **alleviate** future suffering and hoping to arouse in
others his own **fervent** conviction that Europe's wounded soldiers should

15 never again have to endure such **dire** suffering, he wrote a booklet titled
A Memory of Solferino. In the final sentence, he set forth his plan in a question: "Would it not be possible, in time of peace and quiet, to form relief
societies for the purpose of having care given to the wounded in wartime
by **zealous**, devoted, and thoroughly qualified volunteers?"

20 Although the booklet aroused **heartening** interest throughout Europe
when it was published in 1862, it moved a group of people in Geneva to
take action. Philanthropists decided to form a committee to **actuate**
Dunant's ideas and asked him to be a member. During the fall of 1863,
delegates from all over Europe discussed the societies of volunteers that

25 would be trained to aid the wounded in time of war. When one doctor
suggested that the volunteers wear a distinguishing mark as a signal that
they were neutral civilians, the symbol of the red cross was born.

The first national relief societies came into existence two months later in
several German states. When they attempted to go to the aid of the

30 wounded in a war between Prussia and Denmark, however, they were
turned back by the distrustful military. The Geneva committee was discouraged; if the relief societies were going to achieve their purpose, an in-
ternational agreement of a purely **humanitarian** nature had to be reached.
In August 1864, the Geneva Convention did just that. By 1869, ten years

35 after the battle at Solferino, hundreds of Red Cross societies were operat-
ing and twenty-two nations had signed the Geneva Convention. Within a
single decade, Jean Henri Dunant had fulfilled his plan and lifted the conscience and compassion of a whole continent to a new level.

Words

- **actuate**
- **alleviate**
- **beset**
- **dire**
- **fervent**
- **fester**
- **heartening**
- **humanitarian**
- **mobilize**
- **zealous**

Each word in this lesson's word list appears in dark type in the selection you just read. Think about how the vocabulary word is used in the selection, then write the letter for the best answer to each question.

1. Which word or words could best replace *mobilized* in line 6?
   (A) assembled   (B) made automatic
   (C) crushed   (D) restored to original condition

   1. _____

2. Which word could best replace *festering* in line 10?
   (A) interchangeable   (B) healing
   (C) scandalous   (D) infected

   2. _____

3. *Beset* (line 11) can best be explained as _____.
   (A) deprived of strength   (B) selected from a group
   (C) troubled persistently   (D) ruined

   3. _____

4. Which words could best replace *alleviate* in line 13?
   (A) determine beforehand   (B) entrust to another
   (C) move cautiously forward   (D) make more bearable

   4. _____

5. Which word or words could best replace *fervent* in line 14?
   (A) sophisticated   (B) passionate
   (C) having a bad disposition   (D) criminal

   5. _____

6. Which word or words could best replace *dire* in line 15?
   (A) dreadful   (B) rough or grating
   (C) intermediate   (D) diverse

   6. _____

7. Someone who is *zealous* (line 19) can best be described as _____.
   (A) physically or emotionally overcome   (B) flourishing
   (C) extremely modest or shy   (D) enthusiastically devoted to a cause

   7. _____

8. Which word or words could best replace *heartening* in line 20?
   (A) emotionless   (B) encouraging
   (C) gloomy   (D) excessively sweet

   8. _____

9. Which word or words could best replace *actuate* in line 22?
   (A) provide protection for   (B) remain temporarily uninvolved in
   (C) put into action   (D) criticize

   9. _____

10. Something that is *humanitarian* (line 33) can best be explained as _____.
    (A) devoted to the promotion of human welfare   (B) dazzling in appearance
    (C) having a prolonged effect   (D) confined to an exclusive group

    10. _____

Applying Meaning

Follow the directions below to write a sentence using a vocabulary word.

1. Describe a minor illness or injury and the course of treatment prescribed by a doctor. Use any form of the word *alleviate*.

   _____

   _____

   _____

2. Explain the efforts of a committee chairperson to get a project under way. Use any form of the word *mobilize*.

   _____

   _____

   _____

3. Describe a weather forecast that might affect your plans. Use any form of the word *dire*.

   _____

   _____

   _____

4. Describe someone haunted by bad dreams. Use any form of the word *beset*.

   _____

   _____

   _____

5. Give advice to a friend who has stepped on a rusty nail. Use any form of the word *fester*.

   _____

   _____

   _____

Each question below contains a vocabulary word from this lesson. Answer each question "yes" or "no" in the space provided.

6. If you *actuate* a plan, do you cause it to fail even before it is put into practice?

6. _____

7. Might a well-chosen compliment *hearten* someone lacking in self-confidence?

7. _____

8. Would a *fervent* plea be delivered without emotion?

8. _____

9. Is a *zealous* person likely to be tireless in pursuing a goal?

9. _____

10. Is a *humanitarian* likely to be compassionate toward those less fortunate than he or she?

10. _____

For each question you answered "no," write a sentence using the vocabulary word correctly.

_____

_____

_____

_____

_____

_____

_____

_____

_____

_____

_____

Mastering Meaning

From Susan B. Anthony to Dr. Martin Luther King, Jr., people have long been interested in correcting the inadequacies, abuses, and other problems they perceive in society. Write an essay about how you would reform some aspect of society that needs a change for the better. You might consider such areas as education, the environment, or government. Use some of the words you studied in this lesson.

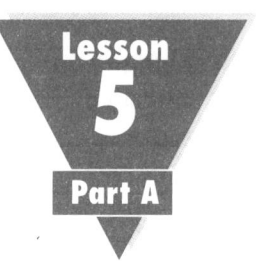

Name _____

In your English composition and literature courses, you've probably learned to recognize and apply many literary terms, such as *exaggeration, sarcasm, humor, suspense, simile,* and *personification.* Knowing these terms and many others can increase your appreciation of literature and improve your own writing style. In this lesson you will learn ten words associated with language and literature.

Unlocking Meaning

Words
appellation
bowdlerize
cognate
doggerel
oxymoron
paradigm
parlance
pastoral
protagonist
vernacular

Read the sentences or short passages below. Write the letter for the correct definition of the italicized vocabulary word.

1. His incredible success and accomplishments at such a young age earned him the *appellation* "boy wonder."

    (A) physical ailments that accompany aging
    (B) financial rewards
    (C) descriptive name or title
    (D) career or profession

2. In reviewing the author's latest book, the editor cut out large passages that seemed vulgar and tasteless. The author accused the editor of using prudish standards to *bowdlerize* her work.

    (A) sanitize
    (B) decorate
    (C) steal
    (D) remember

3. The English word "good" is a *cognate* of the Old High German word "guot," which also means "good."

    (A) word that is unrelated in meaning or origin to another word
    (B) word that means the opposite of another word
    (C) word that is related in origin to another word
    (D) word that is spelled and pronounced the same as another word

4. Some serious poets would never write *doggerel.* They consider such crudely fashioned poetry silly nonsense and not worthy of their literary talent and skills.

    (A) serious stories or poems about dogs and other animals
    (B) literature of the highest quality
    (C) handwritten poetry that does not rhyme
    (D) loosely structured verse of a humorous or trivial nature

1. _____

2. _____

3. _____

4. _____

5. Ms. Sanchez asked each of us to give an example of *oxymoron*. Then she laughed and said, "The 'deafening silence' that has followed my request is a perfect example of one."

(A) combination of contradicting words
(B) loud, unbearable noise
(C) absolute quiet
(D) idiotic statements

5. _____

6. The *paradigm* "drive, drives, drove, driving, driven" is a model for the conjugation of other similar irregular verbs.

(A) nonsense riddle using one- and two-syllable words
(B) list of all the different forms of a word
(C) list of synonyms and antonyms
(D) alphabetical list of verbs

6. _____

7. It seems that every time Janet has a big date, a large elevated inflammation appears on her face. In the *parlance* of teenagers, she breaks out in a huge zit.

(A) friendliness
(B) hostility
(C) speech
(D) indifference

7. _____

8. Although writers often used the *pastoral* to idealize rural life, William Shakespeare showed both the pleasures and the problems of rural existence in his play *As You Like It*.

(A) pasture
(B) artistic work that depicts life in the country
(C) writing instrument
(D) painting that depicts life in the city

8. _____

9. I really lost interest in the movie when the *protagonist*, a timid kind of guy up until then, began to undergo a mysterious change. Suddenly, he was capable of lifting skyscrapers from their foundations and stopping trains with his thumb.

(A) usher
(B) religious fanatic
(C) main character
(D) mythical creature

9. _____

10. When Jon went to Spain, he had difficulty communicating with people in the villages he visited. Their *vernacular* was quite different from the more formal Spanish he had learned in school.

(A) clothing
(B) sense of humor
(C) method of travel
(D) everyday language

10. _____

Applying Meaning

Each question below contains a vocabulary word from this lesson. Answer each question "yes" or "no" in the space provided.

1. Is it common for a judge to speak in legal *parlance*?

2. Are you likely to hear city sounds in Beethoven's *Pastoral* Symphony?

3. If a teacher wished to censor what she considered an offensive scene from a school play, would she *bowdlerize* the script?

4. Would your teacher ask you to solve a *paradigm*?

5. If you played the *protagonist* in the school play, would you have a minor role?

6. If a piece of literature is written in the *vernacular* of a certain place, will it reflect the everyday language of the people of that place?

7. If two words are *cognates,* do they have similar origins?

8. Is the expression "as soft and cuddly as a newborn baby" an *oxymoron*?

9. Is "the absent-minded professor" an appropriate *appellation* for a teacher who forgets things?

10. Would your literature textbook use *doggerel* as an example of tightly structured, serious poetry?

1. _____

2. _____

3. _____

4. _____

5. _____

6. _____

7. _____

8. _____

9. _____

10. _____

For each question you answered "no," write a sentence using the vocabulary word correctly.

_____

_____

_____

_____

_____

_____

_____

_____

_____

_____

_____

_____

_____

_____

_____

_____

_____

Match the example in Column B with the word in Column A. Write the letter of the correct answer on the line provided.

Column A   **Column B**

11. doggerel   a. English word "hound"/German word "hund"   **11.** _____

12. cognate   b. bittersweet   **12.** _____

13. appellation   c. Richard the Lion-Hearted   **13.** _____

14. oxymoron   d. In summer when the bugs are many/I sit   **14.** _____
                           behind a screen/And call to them "come
                           and get me."

15. paradigm   e. the poem "The Gentle Shepherd"   **15.** _____

16. pastoral   f. write, writes, wrote, writing, written   **16.** _____

Copyright © Glencoe/McGraw-Hill, a division of The McGraw-Hill Companies, Inc.

Bonus Words

philology   etymology   semantics   linguistics

For centuries, people have been studying language. This study often focuses not only on the everyday spoken form, or vernacular, of a country's language, but also on its written form, its literature, and its culture. Above are some words that are associated with the study of language.

Cooperative Learning: Work with a partner to research and write definitions for each of these terms. Prepare a short oral report defining these terms and explaining the differences between them.

Name _____

The root *-ced-* comes from the Latin word *cedere,* meaning "to move," "to go," or "to yield." This root also appears in English words as *-cess-.* Another root, from the Latin word *frangere,* meaning "to break," usually appears in English words as *-fract-* or *-frag-.* The vocabulary words in this lesson all have one of these roots.

Root	Meaning	English Word
-ced- -cess-	to go, to yield	accede intercession
-fract- -frag-	to break	infraction fragmentary

Unlocking Meaning

Write the vocabulary word that fits each clue below. Then say the word and write a short definition. Compare your definition and pronunciation with those given on the flash card.

1. This two-syllable adjective might be used to describe a cranky child who has had a long, tiring day and refuses to cooperate with anyone.

   _____

   _____

   _____

2. This noun begins with a prefix that means "with." To resolve an argument, you might give up on one of your points and make this.

   _____

   _____

   _____

3. This verb is a synonym for *yield* and suggests that a person has succumbed to pressure from outside forces.

   _____

   _____

   _____

4. This word is always a verb. A politician would be responsible for all the expenses of his campaign if supporters did not contribute to the campaign and do this to his costs.

   _____

   _____

   _____

Words

accede

concession

defray

fractious

fragmentary

infraction

intercession

precedent

recede

refractory

5. This noun begins with a prefix that means "before." A court decision can be one, and similar decisions are sure to follow.

_____

_____

_____

6. This noun begins with a prefix that means "between." If a lawyer takes this action for her client, a judge might agree to a lighter sentence.

_____

_____

_____

7. This four-syllable adjective is similar in meaning to number 1. A stubborn mule is this.

_____

_____

_____

8. This word is a noun. A driver who goes over the speed limit might be given a ticket for one of these.

_____

_____

_____

9. This verb has a prefix that means "back." The tide will do this after it rises and comes in.

_____

_____

_____

10. This word is an adjective. A mosaic consists of many pieces that are this.

_____

_____

_____

Applying Meaning

Follow the directions below to write a sentence using a vocabulary word or form of the word.

1. Complete the sentence: Effi committed an *infraction* of school policy when she _____.

   _____

   _____

   _____

2. Write a sentence about how a community might raise funds to build a new school. Use any form of the word *defray*.

   _____

   _____

   _____

3. Describe a situation in which a family member helps you get a lesser punishment for breaking a rule. Use any form of the word *intercession*.

   _____

   _____

   _____

4. Use any form of the word *recede* in a sentence about a flooded town.

   _____

   _____

   _____

5. Complete the sentence: In the middle of the store, the *refractory* child _____.

   _____

   _____

   _____

6. Describe how a warden might end a protest staged by prisoners. Use any form of the word *concession*.

   _____

   _____

   _____

Decide which word in parentheses best completes the sentence. Then write the sentence, adding the missing word.

7. By letting students wear shorts on the first day of spring, the principal established a _____ for all the springs to come. (concession; precedent)

_____

_____

_____

8. From the _____ account that several witnesses gave at the scene, the police were not able to piece together what had happened. (fractious; fragmentary)

_____

_____

_____

9. Only after I promised to do her laundry for a month would my sister finally _____ to letting me wear her new jeans. (accede; recede)

_____

_____

_____

10. If Antonina doesn't get at least eight hours of sleep, she becomes _____ and is impossible to live with. (fractious; fragmentary)

_____

_____

_____

Bonus Words

fragile   frail   frangible

If something is easily broken, it is said to be fragile. The word *fragile* contains the Latin root *-frag-*, which you learned in this lesson. *Frail* and *frangible* have a similar meaning and the same Latin root. Although these two words are considered synonyms for *fragile,* there are shades of difference in their meanings.

Write a Paragraph: Look up *fragile, frangible,* and *frail* in a dictionary. Write a paragraph discussing the similarities and shades of difference in the meanings. Provide sample sentences for each word.

Lessons
4–6

Name _____

How well do you remember the words you studied in Lessons 4 through 6? Take the following test covering the words from the last three lessons.

Part 1 Antonyms

Each question below includes a word in capital letters, followed by four words or phrases. Choose the word or phrase that is most nearly <u>opposite</u> in meaning to the word in capital letters. Consider all choices before deciding on your answer. Write the letter for your answer on the line provided.

Sample

S. HIGH	(A) cold	(B) simple	**S.** ___**C**___
	(C) low	(D) foolish	

1. HEARTENING	(A) encouraging	(B) discouraging	**1.** _____
	(C) causing grief	(D) nourishing	
2. ZEALOUS	(A) eager	(B) passionate	**2.** _____
	(C) sluggish	(D) anxious	
3. ACCEDE	(A) understand	(B) obtain	**3.** _____
	(C) refuse	(D) consent	
4. RECEDE	(A) advance	(B) retreat	**4.** _____
	(C) accept	(D) scold	
5. ACTUATE	(A) stop	(B) perform	**5.** _____
	(C) incite	(D) fail	
6. PASTORAL	(A) vivid	(B) rural	**6.** _____
	(C) amusing	(D) urban	
7. CONCESSION	(A) beginning	(B) idea	**7.** _____
	(C) misunderstanding	(D) disagreement	
8. REFRACTORY	(A) unruly	(B) obedient	**8.** _____
	(C) rational	(D) outgoing	
9. ALLEVIATE	(A) aggravate	(B) relieve	**9.** _____
	(C) charge	(D) satisfy	
10. FRACTIOUS	(A) broken	(B) significant	**10.** _____
	(C) content	(D) irritable	

Go on to next page. ➤

Part 2 Matching Words and Meanings

Match the definition in Column B with the word in Column A.
Write the letter of the correct definition on the line provided.

Column A

11. fervent
12. appellation
13. fragmentary
14. beset
15. cognate
16. infraction
17. dire
18. protagonist
19. intercession
20. fester
21. bowdlerize
22. precedent
23. mobilize
24. doggerel
25. parlance

Column B

a. to trouble persistently
b. main character
c. violation
d. descriptive name
e. to become infected
f. showing great emotion
g. example for future actions
h. made up of small pieces
i. trivial, awkward poetry
j. word that is related to another word
k. dreadful or desperate
l. assemble
m. plea made for another
n. manner of speaking
o. modify by removing objectionable passages

11. _____
12. _____
13. _____
14. _____
15. _____
16. _____
17. _____
18. _____
19. _____
20. _____
21. _____
22. _____
23. _____
24. _____
25. _____

Five and Alive

If asked if an animal were alive or dead, you would probably think it a rather easy question. A dead animal lies motionless and unresponsive to sound, sights, or touch. But some things are not so obvious. A flame, for example, appears to be alive in some ways. But *is* it alive?

5   When something is alive, it exhibits five characteristics: growth, development, reproduction, organization, and homeostasis. Compare a photograph of yourself as a baby with one as you are now. To grow as you did, you consumed food and your weight and height increased. If fire is continuously "fed" **incendiary** materials, it will persist and grow.

10   Development, the second characteristic of life, probably became **apparent** when you entered early adolescence. At this stage, your body changed rapidly, but unevenly. Your hands and feet probably seemed too large for the rest of your body. These uneven changes probably caused you to experience some **qualms** about your appearance. If the conditions are right,
15   fire also develops. From its **formative** stage as a tiny spark, it grows to a flicker, then a small blaze, and finally a roaring inferno.

Living things reproduce. The fact that there are so many living things in our world is evidence of this third characteristic of life. One only has to witness a forest fire to see evidence of fire reproducing. One minute there is a single **conifer** burning, then suddenly sparks will fly hundreds of yards and start
20   new flames in other evergreens, which can rapidly destroy an entire forest.

Your body is organized **anatomically** into tissues, organs, and systems that carry on life processes. Our respiratory system takes in air and sends oxygen to every part of our body. Our digestive system converts food to energy. Fire
25   exhibits organization in a simpler fashion. Examine a flame carefully and you will see that it is layered. A welder will tell you that various parts of a flame perform different functions, just as your body systems do.

Homeostasis, the fifth characteristic of life, means "self-regulation." Your body operates within a narrow range of chemical and physical **parameters**.
30   Any time you start to drift outside this range, the body's built-in mechanisms **implement** your return to a normal condition. For example, when you cut yourself, your body takes a complex set of steps to heal the wound. Fire does *not* have a similar set of mechanisms for times of **tribulation**. It reacts strictly to outside influences and does not possess inner controls.

35   Since fire exhibits only four of the five characteristics of life, any assertion that fire is alive is **flawed**. To be alive, a substance must have all five characteristics.

Words

anatomically

apparent

conifer

flawed

formative

implement

incendiary

parameter

qualm

tribulation

Each word in this lesson's word list appears in dark type in the selection you just read. Think about how the vocabulary word is used in the selection, then write the letter for the best answer to each question.

1. In line 9 the word *incendiary* means ____.

   (A) unusual   (B) moist

   (C) capable of causing   (D) fireproof
       fire

1. _____

2. Which word or words could best replace *apparent* in line 10?

   (A) impossible   (B) obvious

   (C) confusing   (D) highly unlikely

2. _____

3. In line 14, the word *qualms* means _____.

   (A) doubts   (B) suggestions

   (C) comments   (D) ideas

3. _____

4. Which word could best replace *formative* in line 15?

   (A) late   (B) middle

   (C) mature   (D) early

4. _____

5. In line 20, *conifer* means ____.

   (A) evergreen tree   (B) apple tree

   (C) oak tree   (D) maple tree

5. _____

6. In line 22, *anatomically* means _____.

   (A) pertaining to the   (B) shapely
       structure of the body

   (C) simply   (D) pertaining to atoms

6. _____

7. In line 29, the word *parameters* means _____.

   (A) outlines of body (B) oddities
       systems

   (C) fixed limits or   (D) tantrums
       boundaries

7. _____

8. Which word or words could best replace *implement* in line 31?

   (A) study   (B) block

   (C) carry out   (D) ignore

8. _____

9. In line 33, the word *tribulation* means _____.

   (A) happiness or joy (B) celebration

   (C) ritual   (D) trouble or distress

9. _____

10. Which word could best replace *flawed* in line 36?

   (A) perfect   (B) defective

   (C) truthful   (D) thoughtful

10. _____

Name _____

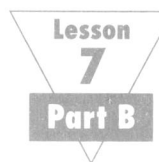

Applying Meaning

Follow the directions below to write a sentence using a vocabulary word.

1. Describe two animals. Use any form of the word *anatomically*.

   _____

   _____

   _____

2. Describe an accident you have read about or observed. Use the word *apparent* or one of its related forms.

   _____

   _____

   _____

3. Tell about your early life. Use the word *formative* .

   _____

   _____

   _____

4. Describe a homework assignment you have been given. Use the word *parameter* or one of its related forms.

   _____

   _____

   _____

5. Describe an argument with which you disagree. Use the word *flawed*.

   _____

   _____

   _____

6. Describe a forest. Use the word *conifer* or one of its related forms.

   _____

   _____

   _____

7. Describe a purchase you made recently. Use the word *qualm* or one of its related forms.

_____

_____

_____

Read each sentence below. Write "correct" on the answer line if the vocabulary word has been used correctly. Write "incorrect" on the answer line if the vocabulary word has been used incorrectly.

8. Most plans fail not in the planning but in the *implementation*.

8. _____

9. Water is an example of a very *incendiary* substance.

9. _____

10. Flunking the English test was only the beginning of my trials and *tribulations*.

10. _____

11. One of my *flaws* is that I can sometimes be snobby.

11. _____

12. The science teacher asked her students to report all measurements in *parameters*.

12. _____

For each word used incorrectly, write a sentence using the word properly.

_____

_____

_____

_____

_____

_____

_____

_____

Mastering Meaning

Write a poem about your growth and development, focusing on a particular stage in your life . Use some of the words you studied in this lesson.

Lesson 8

Part A

Name _____

When writing a story, a writer creates a character's temperament—how that character will think, act, and react to situations that arise in the story. Your temperament, or nature, determines how you will think, act, and react to situations that arise in your life. In this lesson, you will learn ten words that describe temperament.

Unlocking Meaning

Read the sentences or short passages below. Write the letter for the correct definition of the italicized vocabulary word.

Martin's parents would be horrified if they witnessed his *boorish* behavior. He once made a waitress cry when she forgot to bring him a glass of ice water with his meal.

1. (A) rude and insensitive
   (B) well-mannered and civilized
   (C) charming and delightful
   (D) dull and uninteresting

We were offended by the sales clerk's *brusque* manner. She could have been more gracious or at least taken the time to explain why she couldn't help us. Instead, she quickly turned her head and totally ignored our question.

2. (A) discourteous and abrupt
   (B) charming and sweet
   (C) picturesque
   (D) patient and polite

Mr. Hermes explained that the "What's Happening" column for the school newspaper should be informative yet fun to read. He said that the person chosen to write the column should have a *felicitous* writing style.

3. (A) inappropriate
   (B) suitable
   (C) strictly factual
   (D) hidden and secretive

Danielle often lets her emotions rule her behavior, leading her to make *impetuous* decisions. Later, when she can think clearly, she often regrets these decisions.

4. (A) planned
   (B) rational
   (C) difficult
   (D) impulsive

Words

boorish

brusque

felicitous

impetuous

irascible

mercurial

querulous

sardonic

smug

supine

1. _____

2. _____

3. _____

4. _____

Jenna had heard her boss yell at several workers in the office for making minor mistakes. Jenna didn't want to work for someone as *irascible* as he was, so she quit.

5. (A) mild-tempered
   (B) powerful
   (C) inexperienced
   (D) easily angered

5. _____

It's difficult to be friends with Britt. You never know how someone with a *mercurial* temperament like hers will be feeling from one moment to the next.

6. (A) favorable
   (B) predictable
   (C) changeable
   (D) cold

6. _____

Mom says that she just can't understand how Dad, a man who is ordinarily so agreeable and pleasant, can become so *querulous* when he gets sick.

7. (A) happy and easygoing
   (B) irritable and complaining
   (C) prone to asking questions
   (D) puzzled

7. _____

I like Raoul, but I would never confide in him for fear he would make fun of me. His *sardonic* remarks always make me feel as though my thoughts and feelings are stupid.

8. (A) bitterly mocking
   (B) brief
   (C) highly confidential
   (D) flattering

8. _____

"I don't mind that I was wrong and you were right, as you so quickly pointed out," Karla told Emmanuel. "What I mind is that *smug* expression on your face."

9. (A) incorrect
   (B) sleepy
   (C) dimwitted
   (D) self-satisfied

9. _____

The voters believed that they had elected a vigorous mayor who would immediately set to work solving the problems of the city. What they got instead was a *supine* mayor who sat around expecting someone else to take care of the problems.

10. (A) energetic; active
    (B) sluggishly inactive
    (C) mentally superior
    (D) hardworking

10. _____

Applying Meaning

Decide which word in parentheses best completes the sentence. Then write the sentence, adding the missing word.

1. A person who gets angry at the slightest provocation can be described as _____. (felicitous; irascible)

   _____

   _____

   _____

2. Someone who shows obvious pleasure at his or her own success can be described as _____. (querulous; smug)

   _____

   _____

   _____

3. One who does things suddenly and without much thought can be described as _____. (brusque; impetuous)

   _____

   _____

   _____

4. Someone who speaks sharply and rudely to another can be described as _____. (brusque; mercurial)

   _____

   _____

   _____

5. One who shows little interest in ever accomplishing anything can be described as _____. (sardonic; supine)

   _____

   _____

   _____

6. A person who mocks the efforts and accomplishments of others can be described as _____. (impetuous; sardonic)

   _____

   _____

   _____

7. One who makes crude, insensitive remarks about others in public can be described as _____. (boorish; mercurial)

_____

_____

_____

8. Someone whose moods are unpredictable and change quickly can be described as _____. (felicitous; mercurial)

_____

_____

_____

Match the quote in Column B with the word in Column A. Write the letter of the correct quote on the line provided.

Column A	**Column B**	
9. felicitous	a. "I told you I knew the right answer!"	**9.** _____
10. smug	b. "What an interesting blouse! Was it your great-grandmother's or did you actually pay money for it?"	**10.** _____
11. querulous	c. "Let's sell everything we own and move out of this boring little town right now, today."	**11.** _____
12. impetuous	d. "It's such a pleasure to see you. Thank you for coming on such short notice."	**12.** _____
13. sardonic	e. "My head hurts. My neck hurts, too. I feel a draft. That music is too loud."	**13.** _____

Cultural Literacy Note

Mercury

As you learned in this lesson, the word *mercurial* can be used to describe someone who is inconsistent, whose mood can change quickly. The word *mercurial* can also be used to describe someone who is shrewd and clever, quick and thieving—someone like the mythological Roman god Mercury. Mercury was not only a swift messenger, but he was also probably the cleverest and shrewdest of all the gods. Known as the Master Thief, on the day Mercury was born he stole Apollo's herds. Jupiter, Mercury's father, made him give them back.

Write a Paragraph: The planet Mercury and the metallic element mercury are both named for the Roman god Mercury. Do research on both and then write a paragraph explaining why the name is appropriate in both cases.

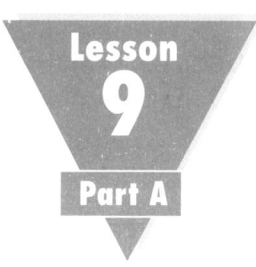

Name _____

The Latin word *capere,* meaning "to take, seize, or catch," is the origin of the Latin root *-cip-*. You will see this root in many English words. It can also be spelled *-cep-, -cap-,* and occasionally, *-cup-*. All the vocabulary words in this lesson have this root.

Root	Meaning	English Word
-cip-	to take, to seize,	emancipate
-cep-	to catch	receptacle
-cap-		captivating
-cup		recuperate

Unlocking Meaning

A vocabulary word appears in italics in each sentence or short passage below. Find the root in the vocabulary word and think about how the word is used in the passage. Then write a definition for the vocabulary word. Compare your definition with the definition on the flash card.

1. As an *anticipatory* measure, downtown store owners began boarding up their shop windows immediately after the hurricane warning was issued.

_____

_____

_____

2. Elsie was intent on starting an argument, which would explain why she made that *captious* remark to Phil about his essay.

_____

_____

_____

3. Michael's *captivating* personality draws people to him like a magnet.

_____

_____

_____

4. Abraham Lincoln believed that slavery was morally wrong, which was why he worked so hard to *emancipate* the slaves from their bondage to Southern plantation owners.

_____

_____

_____

Words

anticipatory

captious

captivating

emancipate

incapacitate

inception

incipient

receptacle

recuperate

susceptible

5. Rachel's sprained ankle will *incapacitate* her for a while, but it won't be long before she's back in action on the soccer field.

_____

_____

_____

6. From its *inception* ten years ago, the foundation has helped countless numbers of needy children in the community. To celebrate its tenth anniversary, the leaders of the foundation have announced that they will sponsor a reunion party for all those children.

_____

_____

_____

7. The home inspector recognized *incipient* signs of termites in the foundation of the house. He said that if an exterminator were called in immediately, damage to the foundation would be prevented.

_____

_____

_____

8. The two boys threw their empty soda cans on the grass even though there was a *receptacle* for such recyclable items only a few feet away.

_____

_____

_____

9. Dr. Irwin explained how seriously ill Maya had been. The doctor said it would take weeks for her to *recuperate* completely and feel like her old self again.

_____

_____

_____

10. In extreme heat, athletes are *susceptible* to heat stroke. To prevent problems, they should drink plenty of liquids before, during, and after a game or any other strenuous activity.

_____

_____

_____

Applying Meaning

Read each sentence or short passage below. Write "correct" on the answer
line if the vocabulary word has been used correctly. Write "incorrect" on
the answer line if the vocabulary word has been used incorrectly.

1. Mom spent six days in the hospital *recuperating* from surgery.

1. _____

2. Members of the women's movement felt that it was time to *emancipate*
   women from the restrictions that had oppressed them for centuries.

2. _____

3. An eerie fog slowly began to envelop Thalia's small boat. She shivered
   as she realized that the fog was an indication of *incipient* danger.

3. _____

4. Doug will definitely agree to the plan; I've never known him to be
   susceptible to any of our suggestions.

4. _____

5. All the patients on this floor are *anticipatory* and are able to move
   about without too much assistance from the nursing staff.

5. _____

6. He held our attention for an hour with his *captivating* speech.

6. _____

7. From its *inception*, the author knew how he wanted the story to end.

7. _____

8. With her *captious* smile and gentle voice, she makes friends easily.

8. _____

9. This basket will make a good *receptacle* for your dirty laundry.

9. _____

10. These helpful suggestions should *incapacitate* the project.

10. _____

For each word used incorrectly, write a sentence using the word properly.

_____

_____

_____

_____

_____

_____

_____

_____

_____

_____

_____

_____

Follow the directions below to write a sentence using a vocabulary word.

11. Use *receptacle* in a sentence about mixing two colors of house paint.

_____

_____

_____

12. Describe a story you heard. Use any form of the word *captivating*.

_____

_____

_____

13. Write a sentence about oppression or slavery. Use any form of the word *emancipate*.

_____

_____

_____

14. Describe a plan to start something new. Use the word *inception*.

_____

_____

_____

Test-Taking Strategies

The Scholastic Aptitude Test (SAT) includes a section on reading comprehension, in which you read one or two selections and then answer some questions to see how well you understand what you read. The questions do not simply ask you to recall the details—they ask you to draw inferences from the information. For example, if the selection says something about the sound of a ball swishing through the net, you would be expected to infer that it is a basketball shot.

Practice: Reread the selection *Cuna Creations* on page 1. Write an *X* next to the statements that might be inferred from this essay.

1. The making of molas requires creativity and patience.   1. _____

2. Cuna men also painted their bodies before the Cuna women created molas.   2. _____

3. Molas are now created by machines.   3. _____

4. Cuna women adapted to the influences of the outside world.   4. _____

Lessons

7–9

Name _____

How well do you remember the words you studied in Lessons 7 through 9? Take the following test covering the words from the last three lessons.

Part 1 *Choose the Correct Meaning*

Each question below includes a word in capital letters, followed by four words or phrases. Choose the word or phrase that is <u>closest</u> in meaning to the word in capital letters. Write the letter for your answer on the line provided.

Sample

S. FINISH	(A) enjoy	(B) complete	**S.** ___**B**___
	(C) destroy	(D) enlarge	

1. EMANCIPATE	(A) liberate	(B) imprison	**1.** _____
	(C) become thin	(D) originate	
2. SARDONIC	(A) impudent	(B) intelligent	**2.** _____
	(C) mocking	(D) meddlesome	
3. QUALM	(A) solution	(B) doubt	**3.** _____
	(C) vibration	(D) dilemma	
4. BOORISH	(A) dull	(B) tiresome	**4.** _____
	(C) rude	(D) charming	
5. CAPTIVATING	(A) repelling	(B) restricted	**5.** _____
	(C) demanding	(D) charming	
6. APPARENT	(A) doubtful	(B) obvious	**6.** _____
	(C) suitable	(D) similar	
7. IRASCIBLE	(A) dishonest	(B) careless	**7.** _____
	(C) stubborn	(D) easily angered	
8. INCEPTION	(A) beginning	(B) occurrence	**8.** _____
	(C) insecurity	(D) conclusion	
9. FLAWED	(A) defective	(B) showed off	**9.** _____
	(C) failed	(D) changed	
10. QUERULOUS	(A) cheerful	(B) sickly	**10.** _____
	(C) complaining	(D) strange	

Go on to next page. ➤

11. SUSCEPTIBLE   (A) questionable   (B) sneaky   11. _____
                         (C) skeptical   (D) vulnerable

12. TRIBULATION   (A) admiration   (B) distress   12. _____
                         (C) small stream   (D) court

13. FELICITOUS   (A) emotional   (B) suitable   13. _____
                         (C) gloomy   (D) gentle

14. RECUPERATE   (A) reappear   (B) retrieve   14. _____
                         (C) recover   (D) replenish

15. INCENDIARY   (A) causing fire   (B) not stopping   15. _____
                         (C) calming   (D) causing rain

Part 2   Matching Words and Meanings

Match the definition in Column B with the word in Column A.
Write the letter of the correct definition on the line provided.

Column A	Column B	
16. impetuous	a. disable	16. _____
17. captious	b. cone-bearing tree or shrub	17. _____
18. conifer	c. rudely blunt	18. _____
19. mercurial	d. container	19. _____
20. incapacitate	e. inactive	20. _____
21. parameter	f. passionately impulsive	21. _____
22. brusque	g. beginning to appear	22. _____
23. incipient	h. changeable	23. _____
24. supine	i. very critical	24. _____
25. receptacle	j. limit or boundary	25. _____

Name _____

Impressions of an Island: Celia Thaxter and Childe Hassam

The Isles of Shoals, a bleak cluster of rocks just off the Maine–New Hampshire coast, are best known today as the site of one of America's notable artistic **collaborations**. It was here on Appledore Island that Celia Thaxter nurtured a wild **profusion** of blooms and from them **distilled** a life-
5 time of practical advice in her book, *An Island Garden*. While Thaxter's evocations of the joys and frustrations of cultivation set a standard for American garden writing that may never be surpassed, Childe Hassam's illustrations of the garden's **evanescent** beauty are among America's finest contributions to impressionism.

10 When Hassam met Celia Thaxter in the early 1880s, Thaxter was already a well-known poet, and her book about growing up as the lighthouse-keeper's daughter on the Isles of Shoals was a bestseller. Twenty-four years Hassam's senior, she enrolled in a watercolor class he was teaching in Boston. Their friendship blossomed when he and his wife **gravitated** to her family's hotel
15 on Appledore. Thaxter became the young artist's devoted friend, **muse**, and mentor. At Thaxter's suggestion, he dropped his first name, Frederick, in favor of his more exotic middle name, Childe.

Childe Hassam, inspired by his father's collection of art and antiques, began painting at an early age. By the time he was twenty, his engravings and il-
20 lustrations were appearing in leading publications. In 1883, determined to become a serious painter, he went on a European tour. In England, he responded to the masterful **rendering** of atmosphere in the landscapes of J. M. W. Turner, and in Paris, he embraced the sense of sunshine and fresh air portrayed by the impressionists. Whether producing **somber** canvases of
25 rainy Boston streets or animated oils of New York's Union Square, Hassam created a **hybrid** impressionism, a sort of compromise between the careful drawing he had learned from engraving and the lush, bold feel of the modern French tradition.

Celia Thaxter and Childe Hassam had few American equals in their time. From
30 Thaxter's accounts of individual plants to her **scintillating** description of her all-out war against slugs, she captured her garden's brilliant hues and her island's wild beauty. In a dazzling series of oils, watercolors, and pastels, Hassam recreated Thaxter's garden in vivid explosions of color ablaze among green foliage or against the gray rocks and blue skies of the New England summer.

35 Celia Thaxter died in the summer of 1894, soon after the publication of *An Island Garden*. Hassam helped carry her to her island grave. Deeply moved by the loss of his friend, he stayed away from Appledore for several years. When he returned, he devoted his artistic attention to the island itself and the surrounding Atlantic. Thaxter's garden gradually disappeared, pre-
40 served only in her words and Hassam's works of art.

Words
collaboration
distill
evanescent
gravitate
hybrid
muse
profusion
rendering
scintillate
somber

Each word in this lesson's word list appears in dark type in the selection you just read. Think about how the vocabulary word is used in the selection, then write the letter for the best answer to each question.

1. *Collaborations* (line 3) can best be explained as _____.
   (A) critical points in time   (B) joint efforts
   (C) obstacles to be overcome   (D) laws that are difficult to enforce

   1. _____

2. Which word or words could best replace *profusion* in line 4?
   (A) conflict   (B) expected condition
   (C) brief involvement   (D) abundance

   2. _____

3. Which words could best replace *distilled* in line 4?
   (A) extracted the essential   (B) moved about rapidly
       elements
   (C) bent repeatedly   (D) suspended indefinitely

   3. _____

4. Something that is *evanescent* (line 8) can best be described as _____.
   (A) effortless   (B) vanishing or likely to vanish
   (C) adapted from an original   (D) artificial

   4. _____

5. Which word or words could best replace *gravitated* in line 14?
   (A) were discouraged   (B) were forced
   (C) became attracted   (D) moved

   5. _____

6. A *muse* (line 15) can best be explained as a(n) _____.
   (A) captive   (B) student
   (C) opponent   (D) guiding spirit

   6. _____

7. A *rendering* (line 22) can best be explained as a(n) _____.
   (A) interpretation   (B) historical chronicle
   (C) disappearance   (D) decline

   7. _____

8. Something that is *somber* (line 24) can best be described as _____.
   (A) sophisticated   (B) gloomy and dark
   (C) revolutionary   (D) bright and cheerful

   8. _____

9. A *hybrid* (line 26) can best be explained as _____.
   (A) artificial   (B) permanent
   (C) of mixed origin   (D) unappealing
       or composition

   9. _____

10. Which word or words could best replace *scintillating* in line 30?
    (A) difficult to understand   (B) lively and witty
    (C) boring   (D) technical

    10. _____

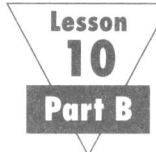

Applying Meaning

Decide which word in parentheses best completes the sentence.
Then write the sentence, adding the missing word.

1. In agriculture, _____ of certain plants produce hardier and more disease-resistant fruits and vegetables. (hybrids; profusions)

   _____

   _____

   _____

2. Cole Porter's upbeat songs, such as "Anything Goes" and "I've Got You under My Skin," are renowned for their _____ lyrics. (scintillating; somber)

   _____

   _____

   _____

3. Business partners Nathaniel Currier and James Merritt Ives _____ to produce color prints of everyday American life in the nineteenth century. (collaborated; distilled)

   _____

   _____

   _____

4. Aware of the _____ of infancy, Ms. Casares put off returning to her job so that she could remain at home with her twins. (distillation; evanescence)

   _____

   _____

   _____

5. Painter Georgia O'Keeffe regarded her photographer husband, Alfred Stieglitz, as both her _____ and her chief critic. (muse; rendering)

   _____

   _____

   _____

Read each sentence below. Write "correct" on the answer line if the vocabulary word has been used correctly. Write "incorrect" on the answer line if the vocabulary word has been used incorrectly.

6. Dr. Hadawe's theory represents knowledge *distilled* from decades of research.

6. _____

7. George Eliot was the *profuse* pen name used by novelist Mary Ann Evans during the nineteenth century.

7. _____

8. Because it was a *somber* occasion, the organist played several lively and merry tunes.

8. _____

9. The pianist's *rendering* of Beethoven's *Moonlight Sonata* was choppy and cumbersome.

9. _____

10. Joan will often *gravitate* for weeks before finally making an appointment to see the dentist.

10. _____

For each word used incorrectly, write a sentence using the word properly.

_____

_____

_____

_____

_____

_____

_____

_____

_____

_____

Mastering Meaning

Whoever came up with the adage "Two heads are better than one" was probably reacting to the experience of working with a partner or a group. Whether you are analyzing a problem or accomplishing a task, team effort can make the work considerably easier and more enjoyable. Of course, it can also complicate an activity if agreement is difficult to reach or if one member doesn't fulfill his or her responsibilities. Write a narrative about a time that you worked successfully or unsuccessfully with a partner or a group. Use some of the words you studied in this lesson.

Lesson

11

Part A

Name _____

Most people do not intentionally lie or try to trick others. Most people are honest—but not *all* people. Skim the pages of your history books, and you will find the stories of many individuals who chose to alter the truth for their own purposes. In this lesson, you will learn ten words that are associated with lies and deceit.

Unlocking Meaning

A vocabulary word appears in italics in each sentence or short passage below. Think about how the word is used in the passage. Then write a definition for the vocabulary word. Compare your definition with the definition on the flash card.

1. When you meet Dan, he'll probably tell you that he has a surefire plan to get rich. But it's just another one of his *chimerical* schemes—a plan like that could work only in his imagination!

   _____

   _____

   _____

2. General Renaldo was unaware of the *clandestine* meetings that took place between Lieutenant Núñez and Diego Sánchez at the edge of camp. He did not know that Núñez was selling army secrets to the enemy behind his back.

   _____

   _____

   _____

3. The jury found the defendant not guilty based on the eyewitness's testimony. The verdict would certainly have been different if jury members had known that the defendant's lawyer and the eyewitness had been in *collusion*.

   _____

   _____

   _____

4. The advertisement contained many *delusive* promises about how the cream would cause the user to lose weight. Those who were misled by such claims found it difficult to get their money back.

   _____

   _____

   _____

Words ·

- **chimerical**
- **clandestine**
- **collusion**
- **delusive**
- **devious**
- **gullible**
- **mendacity**
- **nefarious**
- **spurious**
- **surreptitious**

5. Sasha's mother, who trusts everyone, was about to hand over her life's savings to the *devious*, slick-talking man who was posing as a preacher. Luckily, Sasha arrived and was able to prevent the mistake.

_____

_____

_____

6. Have you ever met anyone as *gullible* as Alejandro? Yesterday someone sold him a ticket to the town beach. Everyone knows that the beach is open to the public free of charge, but he'll believe anything.

_____   _____

_____

_____

7. I don't know why you're shocked that Ellie lied to you about her past. Her *mendacity* is well known to nearly everyone. I always assume she's not being entirely truthful.

_____

_____

_____

8. In one of the most *nefarious* acts of World War !I, Stalin slowed his army's advance on Poland in order to allow Germany time to suppress Polish resistance and execute hundreds of Polish patriots.

_____

_____

_____

9. Although lawyers for the estate of Tyler Witkow were convinced that the handwritten will was phony, they could never prove it. Based on what was probably a *spurious* document, all of his money went to the family's chauffeur.

_____

_____

_____

10. During her conference with James, Ms. Cisneros walked to the cabinet to get a book. While she had her back turned, James stole a *surreptitious* peek at his grades in her record book while pretending to sharpen his pencil.

_____

_____

_____

Applying Meaning

Each question below contains a vocabulary word from this lesson. Answer each question "yes" or "no" in the space provided.

1. Should a bank teller cash a *spurious* check?

2. Does a *chimerical* person approach life in a practical, realistic way?

3. Would a person known for his *mendacity* make a good witness for you in a court of law?

4. Would a spy attempt to enter a military base *surreptitiously*?

5. Could you base a sound decision on a *delusive* faith in something?

6. Is it smart to be a little suspicious of someone with a *devious* smile?

7. If two people were in *collusion*, would they probably meet secretly?

1. _____

2. _____

3. _____

4. _____

5. _____

6. _____

7. _____

For each question you answered "no," write a sentence using the vocabulary word correctly.

_____

_____

_____

_____

_____

_____

_____

_____

_____

_____

_____

_____

Decide which word in parentheses best completes the sentence. Then write the sentence, adding the missing word.

8. Romeo and Juliet were forced to have _____ meetings because their families did not approve of their love. (clandestine; nefarious)

_____

_____

_____

9. He chuckled wickedly as he described his _____ plans to trick Louis and Marcel. (devious; gullible)

_____

_____

_____

10. If you were a little more suspicious and a little less _____, people would not take advantage of you so easily. (clandestine; gullible)

_____

_____

_____

11. While everyone was asleep, the girl made a _____ trip down to the river, where she handed over the map to a waiting messenger. (nefarious; surreptitious)

_____

_____

_____

12. The sheriff vowed that the person who had committed the _____ crime would be caught and punished. (gullible; nefarious)

_____

_____

_____

Copyright © Glencoe/McGraw-Hill, a division of The McGraw-Hill Companies, Inc.

Bonus Word

plagiarism

The Latin word for "net" was *plaga*. Thieves and kidnappers in ancient Rome often used a net to snare their victims, so *plagiarus* came to mean "kidnapper." In a sense, we are "kidnapping" another's ideas if we claim them as ours, so *plagiarism* has come to mean stealing or claiming as one's own the words or ideas of someone else.

Write a Paragraph: When someone ridicules a popular song by recording a humorous imitation of it, the original composer may claim it is an act of plagiarism. The imitator may say it is the exercise of free speech. What do you think? Explain your position in a paragraph.

Name _____

The Greek root *-an-*, meaning "without" or "not," appears in a number of English words. This root is usually easy to see because it comes at the beginning of a word. When it comes before a consonant, it becomes *-a-*. The vocabulary words in this lesson all have this root.

Root	Meaning	English Word
-an-	without, not	anarchy
-a-		amoral

Unlocking Meaning

Read the sentences or short passages below. Write the letter for the correct definition of the italicized vocabulary word.

The massive boulder teetered for a moment on the edge of the cliff. Then it toppled over, tumbling thousands and thousands of feet down into the dark *abyss.*

1. (A) very deep, apparently bottomless hole
   (B) small crack in a mountain caused by earthquakes
   (C) grassy hill used for grazing
   (D) shallow pit

Although we begged Jonah not to quit the team after his disagreement with the coach, he remained *adamant.* No one was going to change his mind.

2. (A) unattractive
   (B) without knowledge
   (C) stubbornly unyielding
   (D) very happy

As a career, astronomy appeals to me because it is *amoral.* I wouldn't like practicing medicine and confronting ethical dilemmas all the time.

3. (A) scientific
   (B) financially rewarding
   (C) without a criminal record
   (D) not concerned with right and wrong

The king had grown old and lost interest in ruling the kingdom, yet he refused to step down from the throne. With no one to lead the people, he feared *anarchy* would spread throughout the land.

4. (A) a state of disorder
   (B) a young, enthusiastic ruler
   (C) calm and tranquility
   (D) an elderly monarch

Words

abyss

adamant

amoral

anemia

anesthetic

anarchy

apathetic

apolitical

atrophy

atypical

1. _____

2. _____

3. _____

4. _____

Ray had been feeling tired, and his skin was pale. Dr. Gregson took some blood tests and discovered that Ray had *anemia*. She gave him an iron-rich diet to follow and a prescription for iron tablets.

5. (A) a condition in which the blood contains excess iron

5. _____

(B) a condition that causes a metallic taste in the mouth from too many vitamins

(C) a skin condition caused by the sun

(D) a condition in which the blood has too few red blood cells

Thanks to the *anesthetic*, the dentist's drilling caused only mild discomfort.

6. (A) angry word

6. _____

(B) funny story

(C) substance that causes loss of sensation

(D) expensive insurance

When Nylia first joined the theater group, she was enthusiastic and committed. She didn't want to be left out of anything. Lately, she seems *apathetic*. She didn't even try out for the latest production.

7. (A) without talent

7. _____

(B) lacking interest

(C) overly dramatic

(D) spirited

Mr. Bramante refused to moderate the debate between the two mayoral candidates. "I'm *apolitical*," he said. "You should have a moderator who cares at least a little bit about the election."

8. (A) not interested in politics

8. _____

(B) busy running for office

(C) not capable of being fair

(D) not respectful of authority figures

After the accident, the pain in Tirrell's leg was so bad that he would have preferred staying in bed. But he knew that if he didn't exercise, the muscles in his leg would *atrophy*. He might never be able to run again.

9. (A) grow stronger

9. _____

(B) rest

(C) waste away

(D) increase in size

The long cold spell was *atypical* for the island, where the weather was normally sunny and warm all year long.

10. (A) regular

10. _____

(B) insignificant

(C) welcome

(D) unusual

Name _____

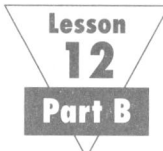

Applying Meaning

Follow the directions below to write a sentence using a vocabulary word.

1. Describe someone who has made a firm but unpopular decision. Use the word *adamant* or one of its related forms.

   _____

   _____

   _____

2. Describe a coach's behavior at a baseball game. Use the word *atypical* or one of its related forms.

   _____

   _____

   _____

3. Use *anemia* or one of its related forms in a sentence about someone's health.

   _____

   _____

   _____

4. Describe a scene from a movie about outer space. Use the word *abyss*.

   _____

   _____

   _____

5. Use *anesthetic* in a sentence about a visit to a veterinarian.

   _____

   _____

   _____

6. Use *apolitical* or one of its related forms in a sentence about a fund-raising event.

   _____

   _____

   _____

Copyright © Glencoe/McGraw-Hill, a division of The McGraw-Hill Companies, Inc.

Lesson 12 — Part B

7. Describe a classroom scene after the teacher has been called out of the room. Use the word *anarchy*.

_____

_____

_____

8. Describe something that might happen to a person who was bedridden for a long time. Use the word *atrophy*.

_____

_____

_____

9. Use *amoral* or one of its related forms in a sentence about an animal.

_____

_____

_____

10. Describe an imaginary student. Use the word *apathetic* or one of its related forms.

_____

_____

_____

Bonus Word

mnemonic

The Greek goddess of memory was named Mnemosyne. This name gave us the modern English word *mnemonic*, meaning "an art or technique for helping the memory." Beginning musicians might use the mnemonic **E**very **G**ood **B**oy **D**oes **F**ine to recall that the lines of a musical staff represent the notes E, G, B, D, and F.

Cooperative Learning: Work with a partner to create a mnemonic for something you need to learn in school. For example, you might try to think of a device for remembering recent presidents of the United States.

Name _____

How well do you remember the words you studied in Lessons 10 through 12? Take the following test covering the words from the last three lessons.

Part 1 Antonyms

Each question below includes a word in capital letters, followed by four words or phrases. Choose the word or phrase that is most nearly <u>opposite</u> in meaning to the word in capital letters. Consider all choices before deciding on your answer. Write the letter for your answer on the line provided.

Sample

S. HIGH	(A) cold	(B) simple	**S.** _____C_____
	(C) low	(D) foolish	

1. CHIMERICAL	(A) imaginary	(B) incurable	**1.** _____
	(C) realistic	(D) friendly	
2. PROFUSION	(A) income	(B) abundance	**2.** _____
	(C) incompetence	(D) small amount	
3. APATHETIC	(A) interested	(B) cheerful	**3.** _____
	(C) miserable	(D) indifferent	
4. SPURIOUS	(A) artificial	(B) genuine	**4.** _____
	(C) filthy	(D) sluggish	
5. HYBRID	(A) purebred	(B) royalty	**5.** _____
	(C) compound	(D) offspring	
6. CLANDESTINE	(A) friendly	(B) secret	**6.** _____
	(C) aboveboard	(D) honorable	
7. ANARCHY	(A) confusion	(B) order	**7.** _____
	(C) revolution	(D) democracy	
8. EVANESCENT	(A) momentary	(B) vague	**8.** _____
	(C) transparent	(D) lasting	
9. GULLIBLE	(A) wicked	(B) truthful	**9.** _____
	(C) obvious	(D) suspicious	
10. ADAMANT	(A) happy	(B) yielding	**10.** _____
	(C) suitable	(D) indifferent	
11. COLLABORATION	(A) isolation	(B) division	**11.** _____
	(C) partnership	(D) ignorance	

Go on to next page. ➤

12. NEFARIOUS   (A) forgetful   (B) considerate   **12.** _____

                      (C) virtuous   (D) evil

13. ATYPICAL   (A) abnormal   (B) authentic   **13.** _____

                      (C) usual   (D) fictitious

14. DEVIOUS   (A) straightforward   (B) accepting   **14.** _____

                      (C) indifferent   (D) dishonest

15. SURREPTITIOUS   (A) sneaky   (B) careful   **15.** _____

                      (C) merciless   (D) open

Part 2 Matching Words and Meanings

Match the definition in Column B with the word in Column A.
Write the letter of the correct definition on the line provided.

Column A	Column B	
16. abyss	a. untruthfulness	**16.** _____
17. muse	b. sparkle or enliven	**17.** _____
18. mendacity	c. conspiracy	**18.** _____
19. amoral	d. bottomless pit	**19.** _____
20. gravitate	e. representation	**20.** _____
21. collusion	f. deceptive	**21.** _____
22. atrophy	g. source of inspiration	**22.** _____
23. scintillate	h. be strongly attracted	**23.** _____
24. delusive	i. waste away	**24.** _____
25. rendering	j. not concerned with right and wrong	**25.** _____

Name _____

The Terra-Cotta Army of Shi Huang Di

Early in its history, China was split into five independent and warring
states until thirteen-year-old Zheng ascended the throne of the state of
Qin in 246 B.C. Assuming the title Qin Shi Huang Di, or "First Emperor
of the Qin," he defeated the other states one by one and **solidified** the
5 country. What was achieved in his brief ten-year reign is extraordinary:
the Great Wall of China was completed, weights and measures were standardized, the system of writing was unified, and a network of roads and
canals was built. For all his achievements, however, Shi Huang Di was an
autocrat and would **brook** no opposition to his total authority. **Maleficent**
10 and suspicious, he had all texts on Confucianism burned and the schol-
ars banished, buried alive, or beheaded.

The emperor was obsessed with the idea of death. Always fearful of some
fatal disease, he engaged in a **perpetual** search for an **elixir**. Shi Huang
Di began the construction of his tomb on the day that he took office.
15 Although archaeologists have just begun to uncover the elaborate cham-
bers beneath an earth mound called Mount Li, historians from the emperor's time left vivid descriptions of buried wealth and **sumptuous**
decoration. What there is no record of is an underground vault, which
would be discovered in 1974 by Chinese peasants digging a well.

20 Excavation of the enormous underground chamber revealed 7,000 life-
size terra-cotta warriors and their horses in battle formation—a whole clay
army, **interred** as if to follow the emperor into immortality. Facing east,
the **vanguard** consists of rows of crossbow and longbow bearers, followed
by the main force of armored soldiers holding real metal spears and dag-
25 ger axes. Surface treatment made the weapons resistant to rust and cor-
rosion so that even after being buried for over 2,000 years, they are still
functional. Thirty-five terra-cotta horse-drawn chariots bring up the rear
of the emperor's **entourage**.

Some of the astonishingly realistic figures are upright, intact, and seemingly
30 poised for attack. Others lie smashed and scattered, the result of looting by
soldiers from the succeeding reign. All of the faces on the pottery figures
have distinctly different features, as if they were modeled after actual people;
like real soldiers' faces, they reflect everything from ferocity to confidence.
The warriors wear tight-sleeved outer robes, short coats of painted chain-mail
35 armor, and windproof caps, all fashioned from the clay. The sculpted
horses, too, are richly detailed with curled forelocks and knotted tails.

The terra-cotta army of Shi Huang Di can be added to the accomplishments that made his reign a turning point in China's history. Its magnif-
icence remains undiminished, suggesting that the emperor may have
40 found immortality after all.

Words

autocrat

brook

elixir

entourage

inter

maleficent

perpetual

solidify

sumptuous

vanguard

Each word in this lesson's word list appears in dark type in the selection you just read. Think about how the vocabulary word is used in the selection, then write the letter for the best answer to each question.

1. Which word or words could best replace *solidified* in line 4?
   (A) made strong   (B) devoured
   (C) eroded   (D) ruined completely

   1. _____

2. An *autocrat* (line 9) can best be explained as _____.
   (A) a scholar   (B) one who makes a loud outcry
   (C) a lover of animals   (D) a ruler having unlimited power

   2. _____

3. Which word or words could best replace *brook* in line 9?
   (A) restore   (B) allow
   (C) express objections to   (D) shield

   3. _____

4. Someone who is *maleficent* (line 9) can best be described as _____.
   (A) well-intentioned   (B) guilty
   (C) committing harm   (D) understanding

   4. _____

5. Which words could best replace *perpetual* in line 13?
   (A) continuing for an indefinitely long time   (B) quiet and hesitant
   (C) imposingly large   (D) outside established limits

   5. _____

6. An *elixir* (line 13) can best be explained as a _____.
   (A) long-buried treasure   (B) small flag or pennant
   (C) medicine believed to cure all illnesses   (D) space under the floor of an ancient Chinese building

   6. _____

7. Which word could best replace *sumptuous* in line 17?
   (A) honorable   (B) extravagant
   (C) intended   (D) carved

   7. _____

8. Which word or words could best replace *interred* in line 22?
   (A) elevated   (B) transported
   (C) restricted   (D) buried

   8. _____

9. A *vanguard* (line 23) can best be described as _____.
   (A) a wide, flat surface   (B) a cultural tradition
   (C) those occupying the foremost position   (D) the place where something originates

   9. _____

10. An *entourage* (line 28) can best be described as a _____.
    (A) luxurious palace   (B) group of attendants or associates
    (C) primitive device for recording speed   (D) stately, march-like dance

    10. _____

Applying Meaning

Follow the directions below to write a sentence using a vocabulary word.

1. Describe a memorable holiday feast. Use any form of the word *sumptuous.*

   _____

   _____

   _____

2. Explain the efforts of a politician to strengthen his or her support.
   Use any form of the word *solidify.*

   _____

   _____

   _____

3. Describe a villain from literature, film, or television. Use any form of
   the word *maleficent.*

   _____

   _____

   _____

4. Explain how a ruler misused his or her authority. Use any form of the
   word *autocrat.*

   _____

   _____

   _____

5. Describe a person's condition following an accident or illness. Use
   any form of the word *perpetual.*

   _____

   _____

   _____

Read each sentence below. Write "correct" on the answer line if the vocabulary word has been used correctly. Write "incorrect" on the answer line if the vocabulary word has been used incorrectly.

6. When the Arabian prince paid a state visit to Canada, his *entourage*
   required every room in the capital city's largest hotel.

   6. _____

7. The principal warned the graduating class that he would *brook* no
   rude behavior at the commencement exercises.

   7. _____

8. The professor was known as the world's foremost *elixir* on Shakespeare's plays.

8. _____

9. From the few bits of evidence left at the scene of the crime, the detective was able to *inter* that the murder was committed by a tall man about thirty years of age.

9. _____

10. The retreating army left a *vanguard* of heavily armed troops behind to guard their remaining supplies.

10. _____

For each word used incorrectly, write a sentence using the word correctly.

_____

_____

_____

_____

_____

_____

_____

_____

_____

_____

_____

_____

_____

_____

_____

_____

Mastering Meaning

History is filled with dictators who imposed their will on others. At a library, do some research on a leader whose brutal or restrictive policies affected the course of history. Then write a report in which you describe this individual's character. List some of his or her actions to support your thesis about the ruler. Use some of the words you studied in this lesson.

Name _____

Comprehending information, formulating ideas, analyzing problems, and expressing opinions are intellectual processes that are valuable in every aspect of life. Whether you are interpreting a poem, debating gun control, or deciding on a career, you are making use of a combination of reason, logic, organization, and evaluation. The words in this lesson will help you understand the nature of thought and belief.

Unlocking Meaning

Read the sentences or short passages below. Write the letter for the correct definition of the italicized vocabulary word.

Carole's grandmother loves to repeat *aphorisms* about people's appearance. "Beauty is only skin deep" and "Don't judge a book by its cover" are two of her favorites.

1. (A) faint sounds
   (B) brief statements of a truth or an opinion
   (C) expressions of complaint
   (D) insults

As senior year drew to a close, Edwardo became more *contemplative* about his future. He began to spend all of his free time thinking about whether he should work for a year or start college right away.

2. (A) characterized by thoughtful observation or study
   (B) comfortable
   (C) unappreciative
   (D) marked by confidence

Before new members could be admitted to the spiritual community, they were required to swear their acceptance of all *dogmas* contained in the charter.

3. (A) controversial statements
   (B) inconsistencies
   (C) relationships
   (D) beliefs considered to be absolutely true

Margaret Mead revolutionized the field of anthropology with the 1928 publication of her book, *Coming of Age in Samoa*. Through her *empirical* fieldwork in the South Pacific, she identified important links between culture and personality.

4. (A) frivolous and lighthearted
   (B) meaningless
   (C) based on observation or experiment
   (D) indulging to an excess

Words

aphorism

contemplative

dogma

empirical

erudite

imponderable

plausible

propagation

repudiate

skepticism

1. _____

2. _____

3. _____

4. _____

Having advanced degrees in philosophy, literature, and art history, Ms. McHale is probably the most *erudite* teacher at our school.

5. (A) exceptionally learned
   (B) important or famous
   (C) self-important
   (D) difficult or impossible to endure

5. _____

Einstein's theory of relativity is *imponderable* to the average person. Without mathematics, most of us can only quote, but not prove, some of its ideas and conclusions.

6. (A) lengthy
   (B) out of the ordinary
   (C) believable
   (D) incapable of being evaluated exactly

6. _____

Renata offered a *plausible* explanation for the recent resurgence of fashions and music from the 1960s: In an era when everything from investments to health needs to be protected, Americans choose clothing and anthems that represent the safety of their childhood.

7. (A) lengthy
   (B) thoughtless
   (C) believable
   (D) regretful

7. _____

Fearing the press would accelerate the *propagation* of rumors about the assassination, the military rulers shut down all newspapers and placed the editors under house arrest.

8. (A) something in an undeveloped form
   (B) the process of spreading or reproducing
   (C) favorable notice
   (D) the act of making compatible or consistent

8. _____

The Good Neighbor policy, adopted by Franklin Delano Roosevelt in the 1930s, *repudiated* the accusation that America was interested only in making profits from its Latin American neighbors.

9. (A) rejected the validity of
   (B) suspended for a brief time
   (C) praised as worthy or desirable
   (D) concealed from view

9. _____

Galileo, who believed that Earth rotates around the Sun, was unsuccessful in overcoming the *skepticism* of religious leaders who accepted the more traditional view that all planets revolve around Earth.

10. (A) extreme edge or margin
    (B) dangerous undertaking
    (C) state of distress
    (D) doubting or questioning attitude

10. _____

Name _____

Applying Meaning

Read each sentence below. Write "correct" on the answer line if the vocabulary word or its related form has been used correctly. Write "incorrect" on the answer line if the vocabulary word or its related form has been used incorrectly.

1. Since early scientists had primitive equipment, they could formulate only *empirical* theories that could not be properly tested.

2. Novelist Richard Wright *repudiated* the Communist Party in the 1940s because of its lack of interest in helping African Americans attain equality.

3. *The Thinker*, a bronze statue by Auguste Rodin, shows a man in a *contemplative* mood, supporting his chin on his wrist and his arm on his knee.

4. Politicians *propagated* in landslide victories often claim that their policies have received a mandate from the voters.

5. For decades after it opened in the 1930s, the Golden Gate Bridge was the longest *erudite* suspension bridge in the world.

6. The use of *aphorisms* in medical procedures was not commonplace until late in the nineteenth century.

1. _____

2. _____

3. _____

4. _____

5. _____

6. _____

For each word used incorrectly, write a sentence using the word properly.

_____
_____
_____
_____
_____
_____
_____
_____
_____
_____
_____
_____
_____

Write each sentence below. In the space write a form of the word in parentheses. The form of the word in parentheses may be correct.

7. The critic's _____ interpretation of the play's theme mystified readers of the magazine. (dogma)

_____

_____

8. For his doctoral thesis, Darryl evaluated the historical _____ of legendary Queen Scheherazade's 1001 tales. (plausible)

_____

_____

9. For many people, animism, the belief that natural objects such as trees and rocks possess a soul or spirit, remains _____. (imponderable)

_____

_____

10. When small computers were first introduced, many people were _____ about their use in the home. (skepticism)

_____

_____

Cultural Literacy Note

Our language is filled with a variety of phrases that express thinking and intelligence. For example, a popular radio program of the 1940s generated the expression *whiz kids*, which has come to mean "unusually bright young people." *The $64,000 Question*, the most-watched television quiz show of the 1950s, now applies to any fundamental, vital question, the answer to which is crucial to the solution of a problem.

Cooperative Learning: With a group of your classmates, brainstorm a list of terms and expressions that relate to thinking or believing, such as *brain trust, bookworm, horse sense, mind games,* and so forth. Consult dictionaries of word and phrase origins to obtain the story behind your choices, and prepare a report or a poster that explains the history of each word or expression.

Name _____

The root *-anthro-* comes from the Greek word *anthropos*, meaning "human being." When combined with other word parts, this root forms a number of words with people as part of the meaning. The root *-theo-* comes from the Greek word *theos*, meaning "god." When combined with other word parts, this root forms words with God or a deity as part of the meaning. In this lesson, you will learn ten words that are related to human beings and gods.

Root	Meaning	English Word
-anthro-	human being	philanthropy
-theo-	god	theocracy

Unlocking Meaning

Write the vocabulary word that fits each clue below. Then say the word and write a short definition. Compare your definition and pronunciation with those given on the flash card.

1. A democracy is ruled by the people. This type of government, however, is ruled by religious authorities.

_____

_____

_____

2. This noun also includes the *-morph-* root, meaning "form" or "shape." When animals talk or wear clothes in children's cartoons, you are witnessing an example of this.

_____

_____

_____

3. This word can be used as a noun or an adjective. It contains the "human" root and might be used to describe certain types of animals.

_____

_____

_____

4. This word begins with the Greek prefix *apo-*, meaning "change." If you think of a football hero as superhuman, you have an example of this.

_____

_____

_____

Words

anthropoid

anthropomorphism

apotheosis

atheism

misanthrope

monotheism

pantheon

philanthropy

theocracy

theological

5. This noun begins with a form of the Greek prefix *miso-*, meaning "hate" or "mistrust." This person would not make a good salesperson.

_____

_____

_____

6. This adjective has a root that means "study." Those interested in this kind of subject might search for answers about God and salvation.

_____

_____

_____

7. At one time this noun referred to a temple dedicated to the gods. Now, however, it can refer to lesser beings. It begins with the *pan-* prefix, meaning "all."

_____

_____

_____

8. This noun has the *a-* prefix, meaning "without," and the "god" root. A person who holds this belief would probably not be found in a house of worship.

_____

_____

_____

9. This noun has the *phil-* prefix, meaning "loving." People who engage in this activity might volunteer their time or donate money to help other people.

_____

_____

_____

10. This noun begins with *mono-*, meaning "one." Christians and Jews hold this belief.

_____

_____

_____

Applying Meaning

Each question below contains at least one vocabulary word from this lesson. Answer each question "yes" or "no" in the space provided.

1. Are Peter Rabbit and Mickey Mouse examples of *anthropomorphism*?

2. Would an *atheist* enjoy living in a *theocracy*?

3. Should someone exposed to an *apotheosis* see a doctor?

4. Would someone enrolled in *theological* courses probably study *monotheism*?

5. Are food and supplies stored in a kitchen *pantheon*?

6. In *A Christmas Carol*, does Mr. Scrooge start out as a *philanthropist*?

1. _____

2. _____

3. _____

4. _____

5. _____

6. _____

For each question you answered "no," write a sentence using the vocabulary word(s) correctly.

_____

_____

_____

_____

_____

_____

_____

_____

_____

_____

_____

_____

_____

_____

_____

_____

_____

_____

_____

Follow the directions below to write a sentence using a vocabulary word.

7. Describe the actions of a real or imaginary person. Use any form of
the word *misanthrope.*

_____

_____

_____

8. Use *anthropoid* in a sentence about an animal.

_____

_____

_____

9. Complete the following statement: My favorite organized *philanthropy*
is . . .

_____

_____

_____

10. Complete the following statement: In a *theocracy,* everyone must . . .

_____

_____

_____

Our Living Language

The word *enthusiasm,* meaning "great excitement for or interest in a
subject or cause," actually comes from the Greek root *-theo-.* At one
time, it applied to the ecstasy arising from inspiration by a god, or to
religious fanaticism. Meanings that are no longer used in connection
with a word are usually labeled "archaic" in the dictionary.

Use the Dictionary: Select one of the following words: *amusing, awful,
virtue, martyr, sinister, outlandish,* and *passion.* Using a dictionary, compare the present meaning with the archaic definition. See if you can
find an explanation for the change in meaning. Prepare an oral report
on the word you chose.

Name _____

How well do you remember the words you studied in Lessons 13 through 15? Take the following test covering the words from the last three lessons.

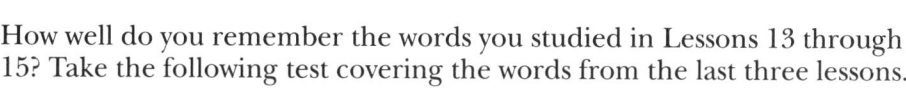

Part 1 Choose the Correct Meaning

Each question below includes a word in capital letters, followed by four words or phrases. Choose the word or phrase that is <u>closest</u> in meaning to the word in capital letters. Write the letter for your answer on the line provided.

Sample

S. FINISH	(A) enjoy	(B) complete	**S.**	**B**
	(C) confuse	(D) enlarge		

1. SUMPTUOUS   (A) ordinary   (B) delicious   **1.** _____
                     (C) luxurious   (D) admirable

2. PLAUSIBLE   (A) pleasant   (B) unbelievable   **2.** _____
                   (C) believable   (D) obvious

3. INTER   (A) bury   (B) arrive   **3.** _____
         (C) hinder   (D) include

4. ERUDITE   (A) ignorant   (B) well educated   **4.** _____
            (C) whimsical   (D) reliable

5. PERPETUAL   (A) lasting   (B) insistent   **5.** _____
            (C) appropriate   (D) temporary

6. APHORISM   (A) trivial poetry   (B) short story   **6.** _____
           (C) speech   (D) short statement of truth

7. ELIXIR   (A) mineral salt   (B) universal remedy   **7.** _____
        (C) delicious food   (D) colorless gas

8. APOTHEOSIS   (A) violent struggle   (B) unusual sight   **8.** _____
           (C) name   (D) glorified example

9. SKEPTICISM   (A) innocence   (B) confidence   **9.** _____
           (C) credibility   (D) doubting attitude

10. BROOK   (A) prohibit   (B) control   **10.** _____
          (C) tolerate   (D) encourage

Go on to next page. ➤

11. REPUDIATE   (A) reject as untrue   (B) approve   11. _____
                          (C) duplicate   (D) control

12. SOLIDIFY   (A) strengthen   (B) refuse   12. _____
                          (C) console   (D) resist

13. PROPAGATION   (A) reduction   (B) reproduction   13. _____
                          (C) information   (D) something owned

14. VANGUARD   (A) protector   (B) conqueror   14. _____
                          (C) leading position   (D) bumper

15. AUTOCRAT   (A) writer   (B) dictator   15. _____
                          (C) robot   (D) expert

Part 2   Matching Words and Meanings

Match the definition in Column B with the word in Column A.
Write the letter of the correct definition on the line provided.

Column A	Column B	
16. misanthrope	a. government ruled by religious authority	16. _____
17. anthropomorphism	b. group of attendants	17. _____
18. monotheism	c. person who hates humans	18. _____
19. theocracy	d. evil or harmful	19. _____
20. anthropoid	e. doctrine accepted as true	20. _____
21. entourage	f. belief in one God	21. _____
22. pantheon	g. resembling humans	22. _____
23. dogma	h. love of mankind	23. _____
24. philanthropy	i. public building honoring heroes or gods	24. _____
25. maleficent	j. giving human characteristics to nonhuman beings or objects	25. _____

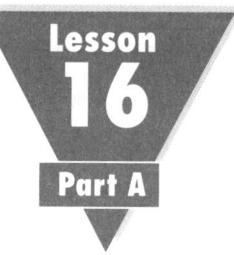

Name _____

Acids and Bases

You have no doubt heard the expression "Let's give it the acid test." An acid test is a crucial, severe test. Acids are well known as burning, caustic chemicals. Less well known, however, are the chemicals called bases. Bases are the opposites of acids. Acids and bases counteract each other on con-
5 tact and are the key substances in many important chemical reactions that take place every day.

If you are like most people, the word *acid* makes you think of dangerous liquids that burn clothing and skin, but this is not always the case. To **assuage** your fears, consider the fact that many acids are beneficial. For example,
10 your stomach contains very concentrated amounts of hydrochloric acid— an acid so vital that you could not digest your food without it. Our diet itself would be very **bland** without acids, because the characteristic taste of many fruits, like the lemon and grapefruit, is the result of citric acid. Vinegar, another common acid, is a prime ingredient in many salad dressings. In fact,
15 the word *acid* comes from the Latin word *acidus*, which means "sour."

However, some very dangerous acids contain hydronium ions, which can rip electrons off of other compounds in a process called oxidation. Chemically, this oxidation process is very similar to **combustion**. Body parts touched by a strong acid are literally burned, a process that can
20 **denude** them of hair and layers of skin.

While the word *base* does not conjure up the fear that *acid* does, the names of common bases sometimes do. Lye, known by the chemical name sodium hydroxide, is one of the **premier** bases in household use. It is used as a drain cleaner. The exterior of its container is labeled with dire warnings and poi-
25 son symbols. Lye is very caustic and can severely damage your skin if you touch it. However, to **allay** your concern, you should know that other bases are quite harmless, and we use them every day with **impunity**. A weak solution of ammonia, used to clean windows, is one common example.

When acids and bases meet, they react, sometimes violently, and neutral-
30 ize each other. Take heartburn, for instance. After someone engages in **gastronomic** excess at the pizza house, it is not uncommon for a surplus of acid to form in the stomach. Heartburn is that burning sensation in the stomach caused by too much acid. The most common **therapeutic** treatment for this "acid stomach" is to swallow some form of bicarbonate
35 of soda, or baking soda. This base neutralizes some of the acid, and the burning sensation in the stomach is relieved. When the base sodium hydroxide reacts with hydrochloric acid, they neutralize each other and form sodium chloride. Sodium chloride is the common household **condiment** more commonly called table salt.

Words
allay
assuage
bland
combustion
condiment
denude
gastronomic
impunity
premier
therapeutic

Each word in this lesson's word list appears in dark type in the selection you just read. Think about how the vocabulary word is used in the selection, then write the letter for the best answer to each question.

1. Which word could best replace *assuage* in line 8?
   (A) ease
   (B) strengthen
   (C) magnify
   (D) publish

   1. _____

2. Which word could best replace *bland* in line 12?
   (A) spicy
   (B) pungent
   (C) tasteless
   (D) exotic

   2. _____

3. In line 18, the word *combustion* means _____ .
   (A) process of wetting
   (B) observation
   (C) method of slicing
   (D) process of burning

   3. _____

4. Which word could best replace *denude* in line 20?
   (A) cover
   (B) clothe
   (C) strip
   (D) cultivate

   4. _____

5. Which word could best replace *premier* in line 23?
   (A) average
   (B) forbidden
   (C) foremost
   (D) safest

   5. _____

6. Which word could best replace *allay* in line 26?
   (A) arouse
   (B) relieve
   (C) excite
   (D) measure

   6. _____

7. If you do something with *impunity* (line 27), you do it _____ .
   (A) under threat of force
   (B) only in an emergency
   (C) at great risk
   (D) without harm or penalty

   7. _____

8. In line 31, the word *gastronomic* means _____.
   (A) pertaining to eating
   (B) pertaining to time
   (C) sensible
   (D) financial

   8. _____

9. In line 33, the word *therapeutic* means _____.
   (A) harmful
   (B) having healing powers
   (C) magical
   (D) expensive

   9. _____

10. A *condiment* (line 39) can best be explained as a _____.
    (A) cleanser
    (B) seasoning
    (C) nutrient
    (D) liquid

    10. _____

Applying Meaning

Follow the directions below to write a sentence using a vocabulary word.

1. Describe how you might overcome the fear of something that frightens you. Use any form of the word *allay*.

_____

_____

_____

2. Tell about how you cope with going to the dentist. Use any form of the word *assuage*.

_____

_____

_____

3. Think of an ethnic meal that you have eaten or heard about. Use any form of the word *bland*.

_____

_____

_____

4. Tell about a fire that you have heard about. Use any form of the word *combustion*.

_____

_____

_____

5. Describe what is on the table where you eat at home. Use any form of the word *condiment*.

_____

_____

_____

6. Tell about a natural disaster. Use any form of the word *denude*.

_____

_____

_____

Read each sentence below. Write "correct" on the answer line if the vocabulary word has been used correctly. Write "incorrect" on the answer line if the vocabulary word has been used incorrectly.

7. Because fuel is burned inside the cylinders, the power plant in gasoline-powered cars is called an internal *combustion* engine.

7. _____

8. Canada is a large country on the North American *condiment*.

8. _____

9. The meter installed by the gas company is a *gastronomic* device.

9. _____

10. Erica had a great game, scoring one lay-up after another with *impunity*.

10. _____

11. Babe Ruth and Ted Williams broke numerous records and were therefore considered the *premier* hitters in baseball during their careers.

11. _____

12. After a bad day at school, I find that music has a *therapeutic* effect on me.

12. _____

For each word used incorrectly, write a sentence using the word properly.

_____

_____

_____

_____

_____

_____

_____

_____

_____

_____

_____

Mastering Meaning

Write a script for a radio commercial advertising your favorite restaurant. Allow a partner to review your script and offer suggestions. Then make a tape of your commercial and play it for the class. Use some words from this lesson.

Name _____

Our language is full of words that reflect size, mass, dimension, proportion, capacity, extent, and volume. Some are very exact words; others tell more about how the speaker or writer feels about the quantity or amount being surveyed. The words in this lesson will help you describe and explain some of the distinctions of quantity and amount.

Unlocking Meaning

Words
capacious
commodious
dearth
equilibrium
gargantuan
inordinate
opulence
paucity
satiate
sparse

Read the sentences or short passages below. Write the letter for the correct definition of the italicized vocabulary word.

Many women insist on carrying a *capacious* handbag. This accessory will sometimes accommodate reading material, a change of shoes, a mirror, a calculator, several business reports, and even lunch.

1. (A) having a prolonged effect
   (B) capable of undergoing adaptation
   (C) strong and upright
   (D) roomy

Although the compact car is economical and easy to park, the more *commodious* sedan offers increased luxury and comfort.

2. (A) spacious
   (B) jointly owned
   (C) snug-fitting
   (D) unremarkable

An unusual spring freeze in Spain and Italy has had a negative effect on this year's olive crop. Even though a large proportion of the world's olives are grown in California, marketing experts believe that a *dearth* of imported olives will cause a sharp rise in prices.

3. (A) prohibition
   (B) shortage; lack
   (C) soft, thick mass
   (D) excess amount

Drug therapy is being replaced in many cases by biofeedback techniques, in which a patient uses monitoring devices to gain some control over involuntary body processes. These techniques can be used to restore *equilibrium* to heart rate, blood pressure, and brain-wave patterns.

4. (A) accepted source of expert information
   (B) one's regular work or profession
   (C) stable state; balance
   (D) structure consisting of several layers

1. _____

2. _____

3. _____

4. _____

By any standard, the Great Pyrenees is a *gargantuan* creature. The head alone of this European hunting dog is the size of a pug or a small terrier.

5. (A) gigantic

   (B) mythical

   (C) economical

   (D) ill-tempered

5. _____

Flying anywhere on the East Coast during the winter can be frustrating. Passengers can expect *inordinate* delays due to bad weather and heavy air traffic.

6. (A) rare

   (B) exceeding reasonable limits

   (C) closely related in time

   (D) planned

6. _____

Visitors to the old mansions in Newport, Rhode Island, are amazed at their *opulence*. Room after room is filled with the most expensive imported carpets and furniture even though the owner usually occupied the mansion only a few days each year.

7. (A) rundown condition

   (B) great wealth

   (C) difficulty in locating

   (D) sensible location

7. _____

Under questioning, the detective admitted that a *paucity* of evidence and witnesses would make the crime difficult to solve.

8. (A) continuation

   (B) regular activity

   (C) distance something can reach

   (D) scarcity

8. _____

Programmers at the local cable station were convinced that a weekend of back-to-back movies would *satiate* even the most avid Marx Brothers fan.

9. (A) depress

   (B) pass off as worthy

   (C) satisfy completely

   (D) seize firmly

9. _____

After a prolonged battle with mange, Zuleika is beginning to look like a Siamese kitten once again. Although her fur is still *sparse*, at least she no longer resembles a bald rodent.

10. (A) not thick or dense

    (B) brown

    (C) intermediate

    (D) requiring medical treatment

10. _____

Applying Meaning

Follow the directions below to write a sentence using a vocabulary word.

1. Describe a horror movie that will frighten even the most hardened of filmgoers. Use any form of the word *inordinate*.

   _____

   _____

   _____

2. Describe an architectural wonder. Use any form of the word *opulence*.

   _____

   _____

   _____

3. Describe the result of an overindulgence in food. Use any form of the word *satiate*.

   _____

   _____

   _____

4. Explain the reason for a shortage of some item. Use the word *paucity*.

   _____

   _____

   _____

5. Use the word *capacious* to describe an article of clothing you or someone you know possesses.

   _____

   _____

   _____

Decide which word in parentheses best completes the sentence. Then write the sentence, adding the missing word.

6. The Huos were pleased with the _____ of their family room but found that the high ceiling made the room difficult to cool in the summer. (commodiousness; equilibrium)

   _____

   _____

   _____

7. Hoisting the armoire with a pulley up the outside of the building required _____ strength and effort. (gargantuan; sparse)

_____

_____

_____

8. The sloth has an unusual sense of _____. Unlike the cat, which will right itself when dropped from a height, the sloth will remain in the position in which it lands and sag to the ground like a sack of flour. (dearth; equilibrium)

_____

_____

_____

9. Pig shaving was once a common practice in parts of northern China. On winter nights rural Chinese would bring pigs to bed with them for warmth, and they soon discovered that the animal was a more pleasant bedfellow when its sharp bristles were _____. (opulent; sparse)

_____

_____

_____

10. Mexico prides itself on its _____ of hitchhikers; anyone caught hitchhiking can be jailed or deported. (dearth; inordinacy)

_____

_____

_____

Cultural Literacy Note

The word *gargantuan* comes from the giant-hero whom François Rabelais immortalized in his sixteenth-century satire *Gargantua and Pantagruel*. Gargantua's name now refers to anything that is of immense size, volume, or capacity.

Cooperative Learning: With a group of your classmates, investigate the origin of one of the following words: *colossal, Brobdingnagian, cyclopean, gigantic,* or *titanic*. Then share with the class the story behind the word.

Name _____

The root *-anim-* comes from the Latin word *animus*, meaning "spirit" or "mind." The root *-corp-*, on the other hand, comes from the Latin word *corpus*, meaning "body." When combined with prefixes and suffixes, these two roots can express ideas related to attitude or physical structure. In this lesson, you will learn ten words that are related to spirit and body.

Root	Meaning	English Word
-anim-	spirit or mind	unanimous
-corp-	body	corpulence

Unlocking Meaning

A vocabulary word appears in italics in each sentence or short passage below. Find the root in the vocabulary word and think about how the word is used in the passage. Then write a definition for the vocabulary word. Compare your definition with the definition on the flash card.

1. The professor specialized in Elizabethan literature, so naturally her library contained a large *corpus* of these sixteenth-century works.

   _____

   _____

   _____

2. No one objected to the proposal to hire a lifeguard for the beach. Needless to say, the vote was *unanimous.*

   _____

   _____

   _____

3. The bankers were impressed with the inventor's idea, but before they would lend him the money, they asked for proof of more *corporeal* assets, like real estate or a savings account.

   _____

   _____

   _____

4. The excited students held an *animated* discussion about the planned field trip.

   _____

   _____

Words

- **animated**
- **animation**
- **corporeal**
- **corpulence**
- **corpus**
- **corpuscle**
- **equanimity**
- **incorporate**
- **magnanimous**
- **unanimous**

5. The blood test revealed an increase in the number of white *corpuscles*. This suggested to the doctor that the patient's body was attempting to fight an infection.

_____

_____

_____

6. An astronaut must possess remarkable *equanimity*. In a crisis he or she must be able to remain calm and rational.

_____

_____

_____

7. By remaining in the locker room and allowing his players to accept the trophy on the field, the coach made one of the most *magnanimous* gestures of the entire season.

_____

_____

_____

8. The librarian told the children's story with great animation.

_____

_____

_____

9. Rather then being embarrassed by his *corpulence*, the entertainer often joked about his size 60 waist and his size 24 collar.

_____

_____

_____

10. The teacher suggested that Rhonda *incorporate* the pictures she took on her trip into a report on animals of the desert.

_____

_____

_____

Applying Meaning

Each question below contains a vocabulary word from this lesson. Answer each question "yes" or "no" in the space provided.

1. Would a *magnanimous* person carry a grudge against someone with whom he or she had argued?

   1. _____

2. Is a *corpulent* animal in need of a restricted diet and increased exercise?

   2. _____

3. Would a very weak person be likely to speak with great *animation*?

   3. _____

4. Would a physical therapist advise you to lift weights in order to build stronger *corpuscles* in your arms?

   4. _____

5. Can one tell that a student is bored by his or her *animated* expression?

   5. _____

6. Might someone decide to read F. Scott Fitzgerald's entire *corpus* as a summer project?

   6. _____

7. Could a private in the army be promoted to a *corporeal*?

   7. _____

8. Is a *unanimous* decision one that everyone favors?

   8. _____

9. If you *incorporate* constructive criticism from teachers into a paper, do you revise it using their suggestions?

   9. _____

10. Would someone lacking *equanimity* make a good brain surgeon?

   10. _____

For each question you answered "no," write a sentence using the vocabulary word correctly.

_____

_____

_____

_____

_____

_____

_____

_____

_____

_____

_____

_____

_____

_____

_____

_____

_____

_____

Test-Taking Strategies

Sentence-completion questions on standardized tests require a combination of vocabulary and reasoning skills. In this type of test item, you must select the the best word or words to fit the blanks and the meaning of the sentence.

Sample

S. In interpreting the U.S. Constitution, the justices of the Supreme Court occasionally must _____ legal principles that are not clearly stated in the original document.	S. _____**B**_____
(A) execute (B) deduce	
(C) ignore (D) collect	

Before choosing the answer that best completes the sentence, read each item carefully and eliminate the choices that are obviously incorrect. Then analyze the structure of the sentence, looking for context clues to the overall meaning. Finally, substitute the possible answers in the sentence and select the best one.

Practice: Choose the word or set of words that, when inserted in the sentence, _best_ fits the meaning of the sentence.

1. The Dutch painter Vincent van Gogh was a _____ genius who cut off one of his ears in a fit of depression.

   (A) troubled   (B) familiar
   (C) partial   (D) secretive

   1. _____

2. Alchemy was a science that sought to _____ one chemical element, such as lead, into another, such as gold, through a combination of magic and _____ chemistry.

   (A) combine . . advanced   (B) pour . . logical
   (C) activate . . basic   (D) transform . . primitive

   2. _____

3. Although slush funds may be used for _____ purposes, such as paying unexpected expenses, the term negatively _____ money used for personal expenses and political payoffs.

   (A) acceptable . . votes   (B) criminal . . includes
   (C) legitimate . . connotes   (D) informal . . increases

   3. _____

Name _____

How well do you remember the words you studied in Lessons 16 through 18? Take the following test covering the words from the last three lessons.

Part 1 Antonyms

Each question below includes a word in capital letters, followed by four words or phrases. Choose the word or phrase that is most nearly <u>opposite</u> in meaning to the word in capital letters. Consider all choices before deciding on your answer. Write the letter for your answer on the line provided.

Sample

| S. IIIGH | (A) cold | (B) simple | S. ____C____ |
| | (C) low | (D) foolish | |

1. UNANIMOUS   (A) unified   (B) alive   1. _____
                (C) unidentified   (D) differing

2. OPULENCE   (A) hopefulness   (B) poverty   2. _____
                (C) wealth   (D) beliefs

3. ALLAY   (A) relieve   (B) intensify   3. _____
                (C) enemy   (D) unite

4. DEARTH   (A) abundance   (B) existence   4. _____
                (C) scarcity   (D) cleanliness

5. EQUANIMITY   (A) difference   (B) composure   5. _____
                (C) agitation   (D) balance

6. CORPULENCE   (A) slenderness   (B) body cell   6. _____
                (C) obesity   (D) inappropriateness

7. ASSUAGE   (A) ease   (B) defend   7. _____
                (C) aggravate   (D) abandon

8. IMPUNITY   (A) purity   (B) permission   8. _____
                (C) freedom   (D) blame

9. GARGANTUAN   (A) normal   (B) tiny   9. _____
                (C) tawdry   (D) huge

Go on to next page.

10. MAGNANIMOUS   (A) handsome   (B) repulsive   **10.** _____
                      (C) generous   (D) selfish

11. SPARSE   (A) dense   (B) necessary   **11.** _____
                      (C) small   (D) uncrowded

12. PREMIER   (A) foremost   (B) mature   **12.** _____
                      (C) minor   (D) modern

13. BLAND   (A) soft   (B) noisy   **13.** _____
                      (C) irritating (D) soothing

14. CAPACIOUS   (A) inefficient (B) cramped   **14.** _____
                      (C) roomy   (D) adequate

15. ANIMATION   (A) hatred   (B) happiness   **15.** _____
                      (C) misery   (D) dullness

Part 2 Matching Words and Meanings

Match the definition in Column B with the word in Column A. Write the
letter of the correct definition on the line provided.

Column A   **Column B**

16. inordinate   a. material   **16.** _____

17. corpus   b. seasoning for food   **17.** _____

18. condiment   c. excessive   **18.** _____

19. satiate   d. spacious   **19.** _____

20. corporeal   e. make bare   **20.** _____

21. combustion   f. large collection of writings **21.** _____

22. commodious   g. lively   **22.** _____

23. paucity   h. satisfy   **23.** _____

24. animated   i. shortage   **24.** _____

25. denude   j. process of burning   **25.** _____

Name _____

Zlata's Diary: A Child's Life in Sarajevo

Late in 1991, Zlata Filipovic, a ten-year-old Bosnian girl of mixed **ethnic** heritage, began keeping a diary. For two years, through the destruction of her native Sarajevo and an atmosphere of **incessant** fear, she wrote about the mounting **atrocities** of a war she could not comprehend.

5 Having read Anne Frank's *Diary of a Young Girl*, Zlata decided to imitate her role model by writing to an imaginary friend, Mimmy, about the start of an ordinary school year, piano lessons, and tennis. However, this sheltered, peaceful life soon became **balefully** dramatic. Rumors of war filtered in from Slovenia and Croatia, and by the spring of 1992, Sarajevo 10 was under siege. Zlata's entries are filled with details about the hardships of hiding in basement shelters; **contending** with shortages of food, water, electricity, and fuel; and trying to maintain a **mien** of normality while friends go into exile and artillery shells shatter her apartment windows.

The utter ordinariness of Zlata's impressions is what makes her diary heart-rending. In one section she notes that the streets are full of aban-15 doned purebred dogs. In another, she realizes that since the war began, she has outgrown her clothes. She is torn between pleasure and guilt as she discovers a whole new wardrobe in an apartment vacated by her neighbors. Her report of a canceled field trip to a concert is matter-of-fact; since there would be 10,000 children there, a teacher fears that some group 20 might plant a bomb or take them all hostage. Zlata's writing is **engaging** and compelling as she tries to keep her spirits up. Only occasionally does she sound **disconsolate**, as when her friend Nina is killed by a shell.

Zlata grows from an innocent child to a maturing adolescent during the course of her diary. She begins self-consciously as a little girl confiding all to 25 her "best friend"; by the end of her **memoir**, however, she has become perceptive and even **audacious**, as when she scornfully comments on politicians:

> It's a war between idiots. . . . Ordinary people don't want this division because it won't make anyone happy, not the Serbs, not the Croats, not the Muslims. But who asks ordinary people? 30 Politics only asks its own people.

The existence of *Zlata's Diary* first became public when parts were published in a Croatian edition by UNICEF, the United Nations Children's Fund. Months later, a French photographer took a copy of the 35 diary to Paris, where an interested publisher pressured authorities into helping Zlata and her parents immigrate to France. The book was an instant best seller in France and the United States, and some of the profits from its sales have been donated to war relief.

Copyright © Glencoe/McGraw-Hill, a division of The McGraw-Hill Companies, Inc.

Words

- atrocity
- audacious
- baleful
- contend
- disconsolate
- engaging
- ethnic
- incessant
- memoir
- mien

Each word in this lesson's word list appears in dark type in the selection you just read. Think about how the vocabulary word is used in the selection, then write the letter for the best answer to each question.

1. Something that is *ethnic* (line 1) can best be explained as _____.
   (A) relating to the height to which something is elevated
   (B) relating to groups of people with a common racial, national, religious, or cultural heritage
   (C) derived from a prototype or earlier form
   (D) having mental skill

   1. _____

2. Which word or words could best replace *incessant* in line 3?
   (A) unnecessary   (B) foolish
   (C) sufficient   (D) continuing without interruption

   2. _____

3. *Atrocities* (line 4) can best be explained as _____.
   (A) appalling cruelties   (B) specified periods of time
   (C) trivial situations   (D) extreme feelings of fatigue

   3. _____

4. Which word could best replace *balefully* in line 8?
   (A) unproductively   (B) threateningly
   (C) quietly   (D) joyfully

   4. _____

5. Which word or words could best replace *contending* in line 11?
   (A) moving rapidly   (B) releasing
   (C) struggling   (D) consuming entirely

   5. _____

6. A *mien* (line 12) can best be described as a(n) _____.
   (A) means of support   (B) casual reference
   (C) behavior   (D) appearance

   6. _____

7. Which words could best replace *engaging* in line 21?
   (A) charming   (B) characterized by close examination
   (C) strictly disciplined (D) foreign

   7. _____

8. Which words could best replace *disconsolate* in line 23?
   (A) coolly unconcerned   (B) expressing a choice
   (C) extremely depressed (D) devoted to a cause

   8. _____

9. A *memoir* (line 26) can best be explained as a(n) _____.
   (A) sign or notice for public display   (B) act of plotting in advance
   (C) prior claim to something   (D) account of an author's personal experiences

   9. _____

10. Which word could best replace *audacious* in line 27?
    (A) ineffective   (B) bold
    (C) inaccurate   (D) amusing

    10. _____

Applying Meaning

Follow the directions below to write a sentence using a vocabulary word.

1. Describe a person's mood following a family tragedy. Use any form of the word *disconsolate.*

_____

_____

_____

2. Describe the host of a television show. Use any form of the word *audacious.*

_____

_____

_____

3. Explain the results of a battle. Use the word *atrocity* or *atrocities.*

_____

_____

_____

4. Describe something that you have read in class or elsewhere. Use the word *memoir* or *memoirs.*

_____

_____

_____

5. Recommend a favorite movie to a friend. Use the word *engaging.*

_____

_____

_____

6. Describe a person's facial expression and what it reveals or hides. Use the word *mien.*

_____

_____

_____

7. Describe an unpleasant sound or sounds you hear on a regular basis. Use any form of the word *incessant*.

_____

_____

_____

8. Use any form of the word *ethnic* to describe a feature of a city or community.

_____

_____

_____

9. Describe a particularly difficult babysitting job. Use any form of the word *contend*.

_____

_____

_____

10. Describe the setting for a mystery story. Use any form of the word *baleful*.

_____

_____

_____

Mastering Meaning

Write a short memoir of a single event from your childhood that you recall or that members of your family have recounted for you. Try to inject some humor into the story and tell what you learned from the event. Use some of the words you studied in this lesson.

Lesson

20

Part A

Name _____

Around the world, people practice a variety of religions. Although they differ in many ways, most religions have one thing in common: the belief that a higher power is in control of the universe. In this lesson, you will learn ten words that are associated with religion and religious principles.

Unlocking Meaning

Read the sentences or short passages below. Write the letter for the correct definition of the italicized vocabulary word.

The church leaders worked for years preparing the official *canon* for their denomination. They feel it is essential that all members have a clear guide to what the church expects of them.

1. (A) prayerbook
   (B) hymnbook
   (C) body of laws
   (D) name

The members of the congregation could not believe that vandals had ransacked and robbed their mosque. "How could someone *desecrate* this holy place?" they asked.

2. (A) handle with great reverence
   (B) steal
   (C) pray with enthusiasm
   (D) violate the holiness of

The director looked out at the young, eager seminarians, and said: "Follow the principles taught by the gospels. Go forth among the people and *evangelize* so that all may know and believe as we do."

3. (A) insult
   (B) preach the gospel
   (C) threaten
   (D) examine closely

A large, elaborate shrine held the remains of the religion's most honored *patriarch,* who had built the first house of worship in the country with his own hands.

4. (A) critic
   (B) follower
   (C) founder
   (D) traitor

Words
canon
desecrate
evangelize
patriarch
perdition
proselytize
sacrilege
supplicate
venerate
votary

1. _____

2. _____

3. _____

4. _____

The preacher pleaded with his listeners to give up the evils of the world. Those who did not, he insisted, would suffer the pain of *perdition*.

5. (A) eternal damnation

   (B) everlasting peace

   (C) exciting adventure

   (D) kneeling

5. _____

The young man was convinced that everyone should embrace his faith. As a result, whenever he was with people of another religion, he would attempt to *proselytize* them.

6. (A) ignore

   (B) share items of interest with

   (C) convert someone to another faith

   (D) pretend to be interested in

6. _____

Our pastor would not allow the dance to be held in the church. She considered such uses of a church building to be a *sacrilege*.

7. (A) honorable deed

   (B) important tradition

   (C) artistic reaction

   (D) violation of something sacred

7. _____

In times of war or other hardships, people often *supplicate* their gods for mercy.

8. (A) totally ignore

   (B) humbly ask

   (C) fantasize about

   (D) command

8. _____

Many Orthodox Jews *venerated* the elderly Rabbi Menachem Schneerson as a great teacher and scholar. Some even thought he was the Messiah.

9. (A) puzzled

   (B) observed with caution

   (C) regarded with respect and reverence

   (D) erased

9. _____

As a *votary* of Buddhism, he fervently believes that he can attain peace and happiness by eliminating all attachments to worldly things. This is a basic teaching of the Buddhist religion.

10. (A) devout follower

   (B) opponent

   (C) free-thinker

   (D) questioner

10. _____

Applying Meaning

Read each sentence or short passage below. Write "correct" on the answer line if the vocabulary word has been used correctly. Write "incorrect" on the answer line if the vocabulary word has been used incorrectly.

1. The owner of the hardware store promised to *proselytize* shoplifters to the maximum allowed by the law.

2. The *votary* insisted on doing penance by climbing the steps to the pagoda on his knees.

3. The bishop asked for contributions so that a *canon* could be erected to honor those who served the cause of religious freedom.

4. Because Miriam and Alice were active in the church and possessed great artistic talents, they volunteered to *desecrate* the new altar.

5. The leaders of the reform movement felt it was wrong to *venerate* images of saintly men and women. Only God, they insisted, was worthy of such reverence.

6. Some early preachers frightened their congregations into obedience by instilling a fear of *perdition*.

1. _____

2. _____

3. _____

4. _____

5. _____

6. _____

For each word used incorrectly, write a sentence using the word properly.

_____

_____

_____

_____

_____

_____

_____

_____

_____

_____

_____

_____

_____

_____

Match the quote in Column B with the word in Column A. Write the letter of the correct answer on the line provided.

Column A	Column B	
7. evangelize	a. "Please, God, answer my fervent prayer."	7._____
8. sacrilege	b. "Under his leadership the new religious movement flourished."	8._____
9. supplicate	c. "Follow the teachings of Christ and the Christian religion as set down in the gospels."	9._____
10. patriarch	d. "God is dead. Nothing is holy or sacred."	10._____

Cultural Literacy Note

"the opium of the people"

Karl Marx, a revolutionary German philosopher and one of the founders of communism, wrote in 1844 that "religion is the opium of the people." In other words, he believed, religion is like a drug, controlling people's actions and deadening their ability to think for themselves. Of course, many people disagree.

Write a Report: The Bill of Rights of the United States seems to endorse the separation of church and state, but sometimes it is difficult to draw the line between the two. For example, should schools be allowed to begin the day with a prayer? Should they sponsor religious clubs as extracurricular activities? Can the Bible be studied as literature in English class? Choose one of these or a similar issue and write a short paper explaining your position. Use some of the words you studied in this lesson.

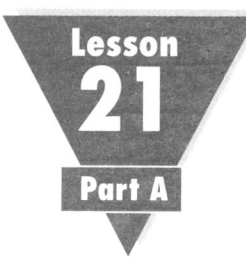

Lesson
21
Part A

Name _____

The Latin root *-ten-* comes from the Latin word *tenere,* meaning "to hold."
When it appears in English words it is sometimes spelled *-tin-.* Although this
root appears in many English words, it is not always easy to see the "hold"
meaning. The vocabulary words in this lesson all have this Latin root.

Root	Meaning	English Word
-ten-	hold	tenacious
-tin-		retinue

Unlocking Meaning

A vocabulary word appears in italics in each sentence or short passage
below. Find the root in the vocabulary word and think about how the word
is used in the passage. Then write a definition for the vocabulary word.
Compare your definition with the definition on the flash card.

1. Tina gets a severe headache whenever she drinks coffee, tea, or cola.
   Rather than prescribing a medication, her doctor suggested *abstinence*
   from caffeine.

   _____

   _____

   _____

2. The judge considered William's concern about missing his flight an
   extenuation, but she did not feel it justified his driving 75 miles an
   hour through the airport.

   _____

   _____

   _____

3. The day they moved into the old house on Elm Street, the roof began
   to leak, a sink overflowed, and the back door came off its hinges.
   These events were *portents* of how life would be in the house.

   _____

   _____

   _____

4. George's *pretentious* behavior can be quite irritating. At the restaurant
   yesterday, he had a friend call him on his portable telephone just to
   make everyone think he is important.

   _____

   _____

Words

abstinence

extenuation

portent

pretentious

retinue

tenable

tenacious

tenant

tenuous

tenure

5. The prince arrived at the airport with his usual *retinue:* his chauffeur, his hairstylist, and his personal secretary. There was someone to see to his every need.

_____

_____

_____

6. The governor insists there is simply no *tenable* reason for increasing the salaries of the cabinet members. She is fond of reminding them that they have had a salary increase in each of the last four years.

_____

_____

_____

7. The baby had a *tenacious* grip on her father's finger. Who would have believed that someone so tiny had such strength and endurance?

_____

_____

_____

8. All the apartments in this building are occupied except the one on the first floor. The previous *tenant* moved out at the end of last month.

_____

_____

_____

9. Although her speech was filled with impressive words and phrases, her argument remained *tenuous.* There were no substantial facts or examples to support her point of view.

_____

_____

_____

10. Many important world events occurred during Harry Truman's *tenure* as president. The surrender of Japan, the U.S. invasion of Korea, and the communist takeover of China were just a few of them.

_____

_____

_____

Applying Meaning

Follow the directions below to write a sentence using a vocabulary word.

1. Write a sentence about a New Year's resolution. Use any form of the word *abstinence*.

_____

_____

_____

2. Write a sentence about an athletic contest. Use any form of the word *tenacious*.

_____

_____

_____

3. Describe the sky before a storm. Use any form of the word *portent*.

_____

_____

_____

4. Use any form of the word *pretentious* to describe something someone might do in public.

_____

_____

_____

5. Use the word *tenure* to tell when one or more events occurred.

_____

_____

_____

6. Describe a young man complaining to his landlord. Use the word *tenant*.

_____

_____

_____

7. Describe a rock star arriving at a hotel. Use the word *retinue*.

_____

_____

_____

8. Tell why a jury might find a defendant not guilty. Use any form of the word *extenuation*.

_____

_____

_____

Decide which word in parentheses best completes the sentence. Then write the sentence, adding the missing word.

9. Without a witness to back up her story, her claim was _____.
(tenable; tenuous)

_____

_____

_____

10. The lieutenant assured the general that the fort was _____ and that the troops were secure. (tenable; tenuous)

_____

_____

_____

Bonus Word

pertinacious

The word *pertinacious* contains the same Latin root as all the other words in this lesson. Similar in meaning to the word *tenacious*, *pertinacious* means "stubbornly persistent." Synonyms for the word *pertinacious* include the following:

bull-headed　　**headstrong**　　**obstinate**

Cooperative Learning: Work with a partner to research and write a definition for each of these synonyms for *pertinacious*. Your definition should reflect the slight differences in the meanings of the words.

Name _____

How well do you remember the words you studied in Lessons 19 through 21? Take the following test covering the words from the last three lessons.

Part 1 Choose the Correct Meaning

Each question below includes a word in capital letters, followed by four words or phrases. Choose the word or phrase that is <u>closest</u> in meaning to the word in capital letters. Write the letter for your answer on the line provided.

Sample

S. FINISH	(A) enjoy	(B) complete	**S.** ___**B**___
	(C) destroy	(D) enlarge	

1. PORTENT   (A) opening   (B) omen   **1.** _____
                 (C) doorway   (D) walkway

2. PERDITION   (A) vibration   (B) salvation   **2.** _____
                 (C) damnation   (D) excellence

3. DESECRATE   (A) praise   (B) use properly   **3.** _____
                 (C) violate the   (D) specify
                       holiness of

4. AUDACIOUS   (A) bold   (B) loud   **4.** _____
                 (C) friendly   (D) unable to hear

5. ABSTINENCE   (A) avoidance of a   (B) stubbornness   **5.** _____
                       substance or behavior
                 (C) serious deficiency   (D) great amount

6. SACRILEGE   (A) room in a church   (B) something offered   **6.** _____
                 (C) false appearance   (D) misuse of
                                             something sacred

7. TENACIOUS   (A) yielding   (B) weak   **7.** _____
                 (C) reasonable   (D) holding firmly

8. DISCONSOLATE   (A) foreign diplomat   (B) confusing   **8.** _____
                 (C) gloomy   (D) religious belief

9. EVANGELIZE   (A) empty   (B) preach   **9.** _____
                 (C) request   (D) make equal

Go on to next page. ➤

10. TENABLE   (A) defensible   (B) easily destroyed   10. _____

                                (C) determined   (D) experimental

11. CANON   (A) code of laws   (B) steep landscape   11. _____

                                (C) large weapon   (D) solemn prayer

12. INCESSANT   (A) harmonious   (B) immoral   12. _____

                                (C) brief   (D) continuous

13. TENANT   (A) trend   (B) stubbornness   13. _____

                                (C) occupant   (D) principle

14. SUPPLICATE   (A) provide   (B) take the place of   14. _____

                                (C) encourage   (D) ask humbly

15. BALEFUL   (A) overwhelmed   (B) ominous   15. _____

                                (C) unit of measure   (D) generous

Part 2 Matching Words and Meanings

Match the definition in Column B with the word in Column A.
Write the letter of the correct definition on the line provided.

Column A

Column B

16. venerate   a. not strong   16. _____

17. pretentious   b. attendants accompanying an important person   17. _____

18. mien   c. regard with deep respect   18. _____

19. proselytize   d. struggle   19. _____

20. tenuous   e. partial excuse   20. _____

21. contend   f. convert from one belief to another   21. _____

22. patriarch   g. appearance   22. _____

23. retinue   h. revered leader or founder   23. _____

24. memoir   i. autobiography   24. _____

25. extenuation   j. making a showy outward display   25. _____

Name _____

Peaks and Politics

Rising straight up from the valley floor, the Teton Mountains thrust into the sky like huge spears. On some days the snow-tipped peaks seem close enough to touch; on others, they appear **aloof** and unapproachable, smothered by clouds. Most visitors to Wyoming who **revel** in the moun-
5 tains' beauty probably don't know that this small corner of the world was once the setting for political upheaval. It took more than fifty years to re-solve the **strife** among conservationists, big-game hunters, dude ranch-ers, cattle barons, lumber companies, and politicians.

The first attempt to turn the Tetons into a national park took place in
10 1898, when the suggestion was made to **annex** it to nearby Yellowstone Park. Cattle ranch owners, fearing the loss of valuable grazing land, de-feated the proposal. After World War I the price of beef plunged, and cat-tle breeders needed a new way to make a living. One result was dude ranches that lured easterners to the romantic West, where they could play
15 at being cowboys. In **retrospect**, the dude ranches sound like an American version of the African big game hunt. Hunters flocked to the area, clam-oring for the opportunity to be photographed with their kills of elk, moose, buffalo, or bear. It wasn't long before hot-dog stands, cheap mo-tels, and souvenir shops **defiled** the beauty of the area.

20 With the hope of rescuing the Tetons, Horace Albright, superintendent of Yellowstone, escorted industrialist John D. Rockefeller Jr. on a trip through the mountains in 1926. Since Rockefeller's very name would have increased land prices beyond realistic levels, Albright suggested that Rockefeller form a secret company to purchase land in the area. When it
25 was learned that Rockefeller had bought much of the valley of Jackson Hole to deed it to the nation for a national park, however, **tumult** resulted. The mountains, lakes, and a very small section of the valley were made into the first Grand Teton National Park in 1929, but Rockefeller's gift of more than 33,000 acres—much of the rest of the valley—was refused. His
30 act of pure **altruism** was interpreted as an invasive attempt to cheat poor homesteaders. Actually, the **vilification** of Rockefeller came mostly from the cattlemen, who were afraid that the Park Service would not allow them free access to the valley grazing lands. The line was—and still is—drawn between conservation and **exploitation**.

35 In 1942, Rockefeller informed President Franklin D. Roosevelt that if the National Park Service would not take over the land, he was going to sell it. When Roosevelt accepted the gift by executive privilege, Congress passed a law to stop it, which the president, in turn, vetoed. Another eight years passed before all the land that Rockefeller had bought, plus the ear-
40 lier national park, was turned into the Grand Teton National Park.

Words
aloof
altruism
annex
defile
exploitation
retrospect
revel
strife
tumult
vilification

Unlocking Meaning

Each word in this lesson's word list appears in dark type in the selection you just read. Think about how the vocabulary word is used in the selection, then write the letter for the best answer to each question.

1. Which word could best replace *aloof* in line 3?
   (A) inviting   (B) remote
   (C) narrow   (D) tough

   1. _____

2. Which words could best replace *revel* in line 4?
   (A) make a demand   (B) shelter or protect
   (C) dedicate ceremonially (D) take great pleasure

   2. _____

3. *Strife* (line 7) can best be explained as _____.
   (A) bitter conflict   (B) several authoritative sources
   (C) courteous behavior   (D) unusual perceptiveness

   3. _____

4. Which words could best replace *annex* in line 10?
   (A) become confusing   (B) add to something
   (C) pressure by force   (D) serve as a substitute

   4. _____

5. Which word or words could best replace *retrospect* in line 15?
   (A) complication   (B) clash of opinions or ideas
   (C) review of the past   (D) random

   5. _____

6. Which word or words could best replace *defiled* in line 19?
   (A) corrupted   (B) declared under oath
   (C) rejected   (D) enhanced

   6. _____

7. *Tumult* (line 26) can best be explained as _____.
   (A) choice and use of words   (B) a mournful cry
   (C) a structure that encloses (D) disorderly commotion

   7. _____

8. *Altruism* (line 30) can best be explained as _____.
   (A) a concealed imperfection (B) unselfish concern for the welfare of others
   (C) a sudden, intense display of light (D) the point at which significant action occurs

   8. _____

9. Which words could best replace *vilification* in line 31?
   (A) denial of membership
   (B) the condition of having been broken
   (C) the act of making vicious and damaging statements about
   (D) an inappropriate or unwelcome addition

   9. _____

10. *Exploitation* (line 34) can best be explained as _____.
    (A) introduction or admission   (B) self-examination
    (C) a series of kindly deeds   (D) using of a natural resource

    10. _____

Applying Meaning

Decide which word in parentheses best completes the sentence. Then write the sentence, adding the missing word.

1. Although Jacqueline Kennedy Onassis appeared to be _____, she was actually shy and protective of her privacy. (aloof; tumultuous)

   _____

   _____

   _____

2. At the time, dumping the factory waste into the river seemed like a sensible thing to do, but in _____ it was a terrible mistake. (restrospect; vilification)

   _____

   _____

   _____

3. Jared, a talented amateur magician, _____ in the consternation he caused his friends and relatives, who repeatedly failed to spot his clever tricks. (defiled; reveled)

   _____

   _____

   _____

4. The valedictorian's soft voice could not be heard above the _____ of excited graduates' cheers and laughter. (strife; tumult)

   _____

   _____

   _____

5. Although Kashmir is held by Pakistan, India has fought repeatedly to _____ the state. (annex; revel)

   _____

   _____

   _____

Each question below contains a vocabulary word from this lesson. Answer each question "yes" or "no" in the space provided.

6. Is someone who practices *altruism* likely to contribute to charities and to volunteer his or her time to important causes?

6. _____

7. Would you be pleased to hear that someone has *vilified* you?

7. _____

8. Must important tax documents be *defiled* with the Internal Revenue Service?

8. _____

9. In order for a business to run well, should labor and management try to avoid *strife*?

9. _____

10. If the ocean's resources are opened to unlimited *exploitation* by fishing boats, could certain species become endangered?

10. _____

For each question you answered "no," write a sentence using the vocabulary word correctly.

_____

_____

_____

_____

_____

_____

_____

_____

_____

_____

Mastering Meaning

Mandatory community service as a requirement for high school graduation has become a controversial issue in many districts. While some people acknowledge the value of volunteering, others believe that high school students' schedules are already crowded with homework, music lessons, athletics, and part-time jobs. Write a letter to the editor of your local or school newspaper in which you take a stand on this issue. As you state your position and defend it, anticipate the arguments that could be made against it and respond to them in your analysis. Use some of the words you studied in this lesson.

Name _____

It seems that everyone worries about financial security. You've probably heard these questions before: "Where will the money come from? How will I be able to afford college tuition? a car? a house? vacation? retirement?" In this lesson, you will learn ten words that are associated with financial growth and prosperity.

Unlocking Meaning

A vocabulary word appears in italics in each short passage below. Think about how the word is used in the passage. Then write a definition for the vocabulary word. Compare your definition with the definition on the flash card.

1. As the victim turned over the $100,000 ransom, he snarled, "Here, take your filthy *lucre*. It will never buy you happiness!"

   _____

   _____

   _____

2. As we drove through the quiet, tree-lined streets, we were amazed at the size of the houses and the number of expensive cars in each driveway. This was obviously an *affluent* neighborhood.

   _____

   _____

   _____

3. Mr. Tapia began to *amass* his fortune while still in high school. He had saved every penny he earned mowing lawns. Then as a college student, he invested his savings in a small computer company that eventually became a leader in the industry.

   _____

   _____

   _____

4. The only *asset* Kendra had was the diamond ring her grandmother had left her. It had too much sentimental value for her to sell it or even to use it to get a loan.

   _____

   _____

   _____

Words
accession
affluent
amass
asset
augment
dividend
embellish
equity
lucre
solvent

5. The college just announced that there would be an increase in tuition next semester. To *augment* the money that he had earned to pay tuition, Jake will have to work part-time during the school year.

_____

_____

_____

6. My grandparents gave me stock in a small electronics company when I was just a baby. The company struggled for years, but it has now begun to show a profit. Last week, I received a small *dividend* check in the mail.

_____

_____

_____

7. Instead of purchasing a new car, Emma decided to *embellish* her old one to make it look newer. First she added shiny chrome side-view mirrors. Then she bought a fancy hood ornament.

_____

_____

_____

8. Even though the house cost $100,000, the bank would lend us only $75,000. The loan officer explained that bank policy required the buyer to have some *equity* in the property.

_____

_____

_____

9. The owner of the Royal Hotel chain was already a wealthy business-woman. The *accession* of another luxury hotel increased her net worth by several million dollars.

_____

_____

_____

10. When his auto repair business showed a substantial profit, Jorge was finally *solvent*. He paid off all his loans and even had money left over for some new equipment he needed.

_____

_____

_____

Applying Meaning

Each question below contains a vocabulary word from this lesson. Answer each question "yes" or "no" in the space provided.

1. Would you consider a piece of property on the ocean a valuable *asset?*

2. Would the earnings from a second job *augment* your income?

3. Is an *affluent* person always a gifted speaker?

4. Would an arrangement of flowers *embellish* a dining room table?

5. Should expensive belongings be kept in a secure *lucre?*

6. If a business is nearly bankrupt, would you expect it to declare a large *dividend?*

7. Might a farmer attempt to increase the size of his crop through the *accession* of neighboring fields?

8. Does paying off half the money you owe on a car increase your *equity?*

1. _____

2. _____

3. _____

4. _____

5. _____

6. _____

7. _____

8. _____

For each question you answered "no," write a sentence using the vocabulary word correctly.

_____

_____

_____

_____

_____

_____

_____

_____

_____

_____

_____

_____

_____

_____

_____

_____

_____

Follow the directions below to write a sentence using a vocabulary word.

9. Describe how someone made a great deal of money. Use any form of the word *amass.*

_____

_____

_____

10. Describe a successful business. Use any form of the word *solvent.*

_____

_____

_____

11. Use any form of *embellish* in a sentence about someone's clothing.

_____

_____

_____

12. Complete this sentence: A college education is important, but one's most important assets are . . .

_____

_____

_____

Bonus Word

utopia

Sir Thomas More wrote of a perfect society in his book *Utopia.* In this ideal world there is no money because no one needs it. Everything is owned collectively. Such a place does not exist, as More probably meant to suggest by his use of the word *utopia,* from the Greek *ou,* meaning "no," and *topos,* meaning "place." Nevertheless, *utopia* has continued in our language to refer to a perfect society.

Cooperative Learning: Work with a partner to list the qualities you feel a utopian society should have. Would there be money and wealth? How would people spend their time? Would you need schools? Make a list and share some of your key ideas with the class.

The Roots -sed- and -sid-

Name _____

Many familiar English words contain the root *-sed-*, from the Latin words *sedere*, meaning "to sit," and *sedare*, meaning "to calm." In some words, this root is spelled *-sid-* and, occasionally, it seems to disappear as in *séance*. The vocabulary words in this lesson all have one of these Latin roots.

Root	Meaning	English Word
-sed-	to sit, to calm	sedate
-sid-		assiduous

Unlocking Meaning

A vocabulary word appears in italics in each sentence or short passage below. Find the root in the vocabulary word and choose the letter for the correct definition. Write the letter for your choice on the answer line.

Every time Molly calls Dwayne at home, he is doing his homework. He has decided to be an *assiduous* student this year to bring his grades up.

1. (A) careless and forgetful
   (B) beginning
   (C) intelligent
   (D) hard-working

The entire school committee voted for the proposed new gymnasium, except for one *dissident* member who opposes anything that costs money.

2. (A) disagreeing
   (B) enthusiastic
   (C) silent
   (D) absent

An *insidious* disease like cancer will sometimes spread through a person's body with no warning signs. By the time doctors are able to diagnose it, the patient's life can be in danger.

3. (A) obvious
   (B) working or spreading harmfully in a subtle way
   (C) well-understood
   (D) affecting only elderly people

She said that she had forgotten all about the argument and that she had forgiven me, but I sensed in her some *residual* anger every time we spoke.

4. (A) loud and outspoken
   (B) remaining
   (C) tearful
   (D) false

Words

assiduous

dissident

insidious

residual

séance

sedate

sedative

sedentary

sediment

subsidiary

1. _____

2. _____

3. _____

4. _____

Copyright © Glencoe/McGraw-Hill, a division of The McGraw-Hill Companies, Inc.

The Roots -sed- and -sid-   107

Madame Flambard promised to hold a *séance* in which she would contact the spirit of Madelyn's late husband. But after Madelyn paid her, Madame Flambard disappeared.

5. (A) comical technique used in film and theater
   (B) performance by female singers
   (C) place where people go to make new friends
   (D) meeting where people communicate with spirits

5. _____

Those two boys are identical twins, although you would never know it by their behavior. One has a rather wild, excitable nature; the other is quite *sedate*.

6. (A) quiet and peaceful
   (B) stormy
   (C) uncivilized; crazed
   (D) similar

6. _____

After a wild, frenzied day at work, a quiet walk on the beach acts like a *sedative*. The anxiety and stress disappear, and a sense of calm gradually seeps in.

7. (A) something that causes nervousness and distress
   (B) soothing medicine or drug
   (C) storm at sea
   (D) reminder

7. _____

My mother spends every day in front of a computer, designing page layouts for a travel magazine. Because of her *sedentary* job, she tries to get as much exercise as possible after work and on the weekends.

8. (A) unable to stay still
   (B) mobile
   (C) unimportant but time-consuming
   (D) requiring much sitting

8. _____

Jesse noticed that the water in his glass was cloudy and smelled bad. He left the glass on the counter for an hour, and when he returned the water was clear, but a brown *sediment* had collected on the bottom.

9. (A) the bottom part of a glass
   (B) snack food
   (C) matter that settles to the bottom of a liquid
   (D) tasty liquid

9. _____

The primary goal of our project was to raise money for a new shelter for the homeless. A *subsidiary* goal was to raise the awareness of the whole community regarding the needs of our less fortunate citizens.

10. (A) main
    (B) unpopular
    (C) unrealistic
    (D) secondary

10. _____

Name _____

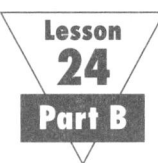

Applying Meaning

Decide which word in parentheses best completes the sentence. Then write the sentence, adding the missing word.

1. Dr. DeVellis suggested that Dad take a mild _____ to calm him after his frightening experience. (sedative; sediment)

_____

_____

_____

2. She received a substantial raise after six months because she is such a dedicated and _____ worker. (assiduous; residual)

_____

_____

_____

3. My sister was hired by a small _____ company of a major corporation. (sedentary; subsidiary)

_____

_____

_____

4. He swore that if we attended the _____, we would be able to speak with the spirit of Abraham Lincoln. (séance; sediment)

_____

_____

_____

5. Even after the winds and rains had stopped, the _____ effects of Hurricane Hugo were felt for months. (dissident; residual)

_____

_____

_____

6. There was a rocky _____ all along the bottom of the river that Dad said had been deposited by a glacier. (sedative; sediment)

_____

_____

_____

7. Because I get restless if I sit for more than an hour, I could never be happy at a _____ job. (sedentary; subsidiary)

_____

_____

_____

8. An _____ rumor, based on lies, ruined his political career. (assiduous; insidious)

_____

_____

_____

9. The office was in total chaos, but Mr. Peterson, who had recently started taking a relaxation techniques class, remained _____. (insidious; sedate)

_____

_____

_____

10. The meeting was disturbed by the _____ comments of a heckler sitting in the back of the room. (dissident, residual)

_____

_____

_____

Our Living Language

back-formation

Back-formation is the process of forming words by removing a prefix or suffix from another word. For example, *sedate* is a back-formation of *sedative*.

Create New Words: Use the process of back-formation to create words for the following. Check your answers in the dictionary.

to show enthusiasm

to commit burglary

to broadcast on television

to learn through intuition

Name _____

How well do you remember the words you studied in Lessons 22 through 24? Take the following test covering the words from the last three lessons.

Part 1 Antonyms

Each question below includes a word in capital letters, followed by four words or phrases. Choose the word or phrase that is most nearly <u>opposite</u> in meaning to the word in capital letters. Consider all choices before deciding on your answer. Write the letter for your answer on the line provided.

Sample

S. HIGH	(A) cold	(B) simple	**S.** ___C___
	(C) low	(D) foolish	

1. SEDENTARY	(A) motionless	(B) soothing	**1.** _____
	(C) active	(D) heavily guarded	
2. AFFLUENT	(A) impoverished	(B) wealthy	**2.** _____
	(C) influential	(D) awkward	
3. ALTRUISM	(A) godlessness	(B) falsehood	**3.** _____
	(C) friendliness	(D) selfishness	
4. ASSIDUOUS	(A) incompetent	(B) lazy	**4.** _____
	(C) diligent	(D) hesitant	
5. AMASS	(A) collect	(B) bore	**5.** _____
	(C) modify	(D) scatter	
6. DEFILE	(A) respect	(B) sharpen	**6.** _____
	(C) insult	(D) imitate	
7. SEDATE	(A) uncertain	(B) drab	**7.** _____
	(C) excitable	(D) dignified	
8. EMBELLISH	(A) compensate	(B) simplify	**8.** _____
	(C) decorate	(D) shame	
9. ANNEX	(A) condemn	(B) secure	**9.** _____
	(C) suspend	(D) disconnect	
10. DISSIDENT	(A) agreeable	(B) prohibited	**10.** _____
	(C) religious	(D) satisfying	

Go on to next page. ➤

11. AUGMENT   (A) repel   (B) permit   11. _____
                        (C) reject   (D) diminish

12. STRIFE   (A) conflict   (B) renewal   12. _____
                        (C) harmony   (D) imagination

13. INSIDIOUS   (A) amusing   (B) treacherous   13. _____
                        (C) forthright   (D) demanding

14. ASSET   (A) discomfort   (B) money   14. _____
                        (C) deny   (D) liability

15. VILIFICATION   (A) praise   (B) blame   15. _____
                        (C) extension   (D) education

Part 2 Matching Words and Meanings

Match the definition in Column B with the word in Column A.
Write the letter of the correct definition on the line provided.

Column A	Column B	
16. equity	a. money or profits	16. _____
17. residual	b. calming medication	17. _____
18. retrospect	c. a share of the profits of a company	18. _____
19. sediment	d. remaining	19. _____
20. lucre	e. distant	20. _____
21. aloof	f. matter that settles to the bottom of a liquid	21. _____
22. solvent	g. able to pay one's debts	22. _____
23. sedative	h. reexamination of the past	23. _____
24. revel	i. take great pleasure	24. _____
25. dividend	j. value of property after debts are subtracted	25. _____

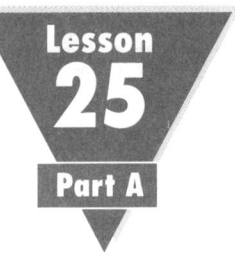

Name _____

Charting the Elements

Throughout history, people have wondered about the composition of the earth and of the air around them. Early explanations tended to be more philosophical than scientific. Aristotle held that everything was made of just four substances—earth, air, fire, and water. This belief persisted for
5 more than two thousand years and is mentioned in numerous essays, poems, and other writings. However, when this theory was examined scientifically, it was shown to be **unfounded**.

In the fourth and fifth centuries, a peculiar combination of myth, magic, and science began to gain prominence. Developed by the Chinese and
10 Egyptians, **alchemy** soon became popular in various parts of the world, although some Christians rejected it as the work of **infidels**. Many of the alchemists' efforts were devoted to a **futile** search for a method of turning common metals into gold. Although such efforts seem rather far removed from science as we know it today, some scientific knowledge was
15 eventually **extrapolated** from alchemy.

It was not until the nineteenth century that the **ascendancy** of modern chemistry began. One of the first to see patterns in the reactions of elements was a German chemist named Dobereiner. He noted that certain elements with similar properties occurred in groups of threes, which he
20 called triads. Dobereiner's **rudimentary** observations set off a search for more relationships, and in 1866 an English chemist named Newlands proposed his law of octaves, which **superseded** Dobereiner's triads. Newlands noticed that if elements were arranged in order of weight, certain characteristics reappeared with every eighth element. With this discovery,
25 Newlands could now predict the properties of a hypothetical element even before it was discovered.

Three years later a Russian scientist, Dmitri Mendeleev, refined Newlands's observations. Mendeleev also had observed that certain properties seemed to recur on a regular basis. His special contribution, how-
30 ever, was his unique way of demonstrating this cycle. Without resorting to scientific **lingo** or confusing mathematics, he devised a chart of the elements, arranged in order of weight, that could be understood by almost anyone. Moreover, he took the unusual step of leaving certain parts of the chart blank. An empty place indicated that an element of a certain weight
35 and property existed theoretically, but to date such an element had not been found. Chemistry then became not only the study of existing matter, but a means of predicting future discoveries.

Today, in almost any scientific laboratory in the world, the periodic table of the elements is **blazoned** on the wall — an enduring tribute to the work
40 of Dmitri Mendeleev.

Words

- **alchemy**
- **ascendancy**
- **blazon**
- **extrapolate**
- **futile**
- **infidel**
- **lingo**
- **rudimentary**
- **supersede**
- **unfounded**

Each word in this lesson's word list appears in dark type in the selection you just read. Think about how the vocabulary word is used in the selection, then write the letter for the best answer to each question.

1. An *unfounded* theory (line 7) is one that is _____.
   (A) not based on fact   (B) highly regarded
   (C) pleasing to the touch (D) related to the solar system

   1. _____

2. In line 10, *alchemy* means _____.
   (A) any foreign land   (B) medieval chemical philosophy
   (C) popular literature   (D) modern science

   2. _____

3. An *infidel* (line 11) is a(n) _____.
   (A) person without   (B) expert
       religious beliefs
   (C) chemical compound   (D) colorful demonstration

   3. _____

4. In line 12 the word *futile* means _____.
   (A) successful   (B) humorous
   (C) expensive   (D) ineffective

   4. _____

5. In line 15, *extrapolated* means _____.
   (A) hidden   (B) reasoned by extending
                                 known information
   (C) evaporated   (D) discarded

   5. _____

6. In line 16, *ascendancy* means _____.
   (A) embarrassment   (B) diminishing importance
   (C) royal approval   (D) dominance

   6. _____

7. Which word could best replace *rudimentary* in line 20?
   (A) foolish   (B) advanced
   (C) insulting   (D) elementary

   7. _____

8. In line 22, *superseded* means _____.
   (A) ignored   (B) replaced
   (C) satisfied   (D) explored

   8. _____

9. Which word or words could best replace *lingo* in line 31?
   (A) stories   (B) tricks
   (C) specialized vocabulary (D) proofs

   9. _____

10. In line 39, *blazoned* means _____.
    (A) displayed   (B) carefully hidden
    (C) specialized vocabulary (D) disguised

    10. _____

Applying Meaning

Follow the directions below to write a sentence using a vocabulary word.

1. Describe a ridiculous chemistry experiment. Use any form of the word *alchemy* .

   _____

   _____

   _____

2. Use any form of the word *ascendancy* to describe a trend that appears to be occurring somewhere in the world.

   _____

   _____

   _____

3. Think of a structure or display in your town and describe it. Use any form of the word *blazon*.

   _____

   _____

   _____

4. Tell about something you or someone you know tried without success. Use any form of the word *futile*.

   _____

   _____

   _____

5. Use *lingo* in a sentence about computers.

   _____

   _____

   _____

6. Write a sentence about a rumor. Use the word *unfounded*.

   _____

   _____

   _____

7. Tell about a new law or regulation. Use any form of the word *supersede*.

_____

_____

_____

Read each sentence below. Write "correct" on the answer line if the vocabulary word has been used correctly. Write "incorrect" on the answer line if the vocabulary word has been used incorrectly.

8. Because the bees were constantly buzzing about, it was difficult to *extrapolate* the honey from the hive.

8. _____

9. I thought that the host's *rudimentary* comments were quite offensive.

9. _____

10. The missionaries wanted to bring their faith to the *infidels*.

10. _____

11. Attempts to revive interest in the proposed legislation proved *futile* and eventually the bill died in committee.

11. _____

12. The general indicated that his orders *superseded* any his troops may have received from lower officers.

12. _____

For each word used incorrectly, write a sentence using the vocabulary word properly.

_____

_____

_____

_____

_____

_____

_____

Mastering Meaning

Chemistry affects our lives in ways we often do not realize. The chlorine used in swimming pools, the solutions used to clean our houses, and the sprays used to treat our lawns all have their basis in chemistry. A large company at one time used the slogan "Better living through chemistry." Do you agree that chemistry makes our lives better? Does it have some serious disadvantages? Write a short paper giving one example of how chemistry has affected your life positively or negatively. Use some words from this lesson.

Name _____

Do you enjoy solving mysteries? A good mystery story challenges your mind. You have to pay close attention to all the clues. Then you have to put all the clues together to solve the mystery. This is what makes mysteries so much fun. In this lesson, you will learn ten words that are associated with mysteries, riddles, and puzzling problems.

Unlocking Meaning

Read the short passages below. Write the letter for the correct definition of the italicized vocabulary word.

Are you familiar with the *conundrum* "When is a door not a door?" The answer, by the way, is "When it's ajar."

1. (A) riddle answered with a play on words
(B) musical instrument
(C) popular slogan
(D) opening into a room

The witness tried to explain the situation to the two police officers. However, her explanation was so *convoluted* that the police could not follow her story.

2. (A) short
(B) simple and straightforward
(C) funny
(D) complicated

Just before Gina climbed into the cab, she turned and made a *cryptic* remark about Dr. Mallorca. We were still wondering what her strange comment meant long after we got home.

3. (A) flattering
(B) mysterious
(C) lengthy
(D) sad

Mr. Starsky was an excellent, dedicated teacher whom everyone liked and admired. Why he suddenly quit his job and enlisted in the army is an *enigma* to the entire community.

4. (A) obvious conclusion
(B) valid reason
(C) admirable quality
(D) something that is hard to understand

Words
conundrum
convoluted
cryptic
enigma
ineffable
labyrinth
numinous
perplex
quandary
soluble

1. _____

2. _____

3. _____

4. _____

The woman's joy upon learning that her son had been rescued was *ineffable*. She could not find words to express her extreme happiness or her gratitude to the firefighters.

5. (A) carefully concealed

    (B) without feeling

    (C) indescribable

    (D) temporary

5. _____

The first time Deirdre explored the winding tunnels in the big old house, she got lost. After that, whenever she went down into that dark *labyrinth*, she left bright markers along the way to help her find her way out.

6. (A) maze

    (B) laboratory

    (C) brightly lit room

    (D) well-marked trail

6. _____

Some people believe that the abandoned castle on the hill is haunted by the ghost of its murdered owner. Personally, I think someone made up that story to make the town famous. It's silly to think anything *numinous* is responsible for the noises.

7. (A) friendly

    (B) supernatural

    (C) frozen

    (D) related to money

7. _____

The lack of clues at the crime scene seemed to *perplex* everyone but the veteran detective. Within three weeks, he unraveled the mystery and arrested a suspect.

8. (A) cause excitement

    (B) greatly amuse

    (C) confuse and bewilder

    (D) clarify

8. _____

Jan was in a *quandary* over the money she found. She needed the money for school clothes, but if she kept it, her conscience would bother her terribly.

9. (A) unfamiliar location

    (B) clear state of mind

    (C) state of joy

    (D) state of doubt

9. _____

After struggling for days to decode the message, most of the members of the committee wanted to give up. But the chairperson insisted that the problem was *soluble,* so the work continued.

10. (A) able to be solved

    (B) able to be made solid

    (C) in a secure position

    (D) unreadable

10. _____

Applying Meaning

Read each sentence or short passage below. Write "correct" on the answer line if the vocabulary word has been used correctly. Write "incorrect" on the answer line if the vocabulary word has been used incorrectly.

1. Santos is in a *quandary* over whether to finish college or to accept a huge salary to play professional baseball.

    1. _____

2. The x-ray revealed a small *enigma*. Fortunately, the doctor was able to remove it with just minor surgery.

    2. _____

3. The manager said that in the event of a sudden *conundrum*, we should leave the hotel quickly, using the back stairway.

    3. _____

4. After we moved into the house on Aspen Street, weird things began to happen. There had been rumors of *numinous* occurrences at the place, but we hadn't paid any attention to them.

    4. _____

5. The map was confusing, and soon we were lost in a *labyrinth* of narrow winding streets and alleys.

    5. _____

6. The carpenter assured us that the wall was well constructed and would be *soluble* for years to come.

    6. _____

7. With a *cryptic* "Write a last letter to your parents," the camp counselor welcomed us to the training site.

    7. _____

For each word used incorrectly, write a sentence using the word properly.

_____

_____

_____

_____

_____

_____

_____

_____

_____

_____

_____

_____

_____

_____

_____

Follow the directions below to write a sentence using a vocabulary word.

8. Write a sentence about a strong feeling someone had. Use the word *ineffable*.

_____

_____

_____

9. Describe something you read in a textbook or magazine. Use the word *convoluted*.

_____

_____

_____

10. Write a sentence about a missing key. Use any form of the word *perplex*.

_____

_____

_____

Cultural Literacy Note

The Riddle of the Sphinx

In Greek mythology, the Sphinx was a winged creature with a lion's body and a woman's head. According to legend, this monstrous beast would ambush travelers on the road to Thebes and ask them a riddle. If they could not solve the riddle, the Sphinx killed them. The riddle goes like this: What walks on four legs, then two legs, then three legs?

Cooperative Learning: Work with a partner to find the answer to the riddle of the Sphinx. Then write a paragraph that gives some background about the person in Greek mythology who finally solved the riddle.

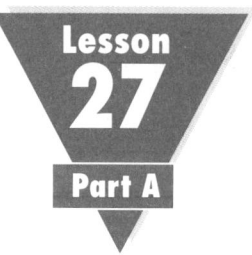

Lesson
27
Part A

Name _____

The root *-duc-*, from the Latin word *ducere,* means "to lead," and appears in many familiar English words. The root *-reg-*, from the Latin word *regere,* means "to rule." Each vocabulary word in this lesson has one of these roots.

Root	Meaning	English Word
-duc-	to lead	abduct
-reg-	to rule	regimen

Unlocking Meaning

A vocabulary word appears in italics in each sentence or short passage below. Find the root in the vocabulary word and think about how the word is used in the passage. Then write a definition for the vocabulary word. Compare your definition with the definition on the flash card.

Words

abduct

adduce

deduce

educe

regalia

regime

regimen

regiment

regnant

seduce

1. Two men tried to *abduct* the wealthy diamond merchant in the hope of demanding a huge ransom for her return.

_____

_____

_____

2. The drop in the crime rate was quite dramatic after additional police officers were hired. The mayor plans to *adduce* these statistics when he proposes that additional officers be added to the force.

_____

_____

_____

3. By checking the telephone company's records, the attorney was able to *deduce* that his client had been at home all day and therefore could not have committed the robbery.

_____

_____

_____

4. Mae's acting skills had remained hidden beneath her shy exterior. It took the gentle coaxing of the play's director to *educe* her talent.

_____

_____

_____

5. The king dressed in full *regalia* to meet with members of parliament. After donning his purple velvet cape and putting on his crown, he grasped the royal scepter and approached the door of the chamber.

_____

_____

_____

6. Under the old *regime*, thousands of people suffered from a multitude of human rights abuses. The new leaders, however, promised to re-spect and protect the rights of all citizens.

_____

_____

_____

7. Pablo follows a strict fitness *regimen*. Every weekday, he gets up at 6:30 and runs five miles. At noon, he works out at the gym for an hour. Then, after work, he rides his bike at least ten miles.

_____

_____

_____

8. Looking over the new class of freshmen, the headmaster of the school shook his head in disbelief. This latest group was poorly groomed and completely undisciplined. Attempting to *regiment* this collection of misfits would not be easy.

_____

_____

_____

9. As the *regnant* queen, she enjoyed the love, adoration, and utmost respect of her subjects. Now that she has stepped down from the throne and handed power over to her son, she is still beloved by all.

_____

_____

_____

10. By making the advertisement look like a notice that I had won a valu-able prize, the promoters *seduced* me into sending money for a maga-zine subscription.

_____

_____

_____

Applying Meaning

Decide which word in parentheses best completes the sentence. Then write the sentence, adding the missing word.

1. The ambassadors dressed in their formal _____ for the state dinner at the White House. (regalia; regiment)

   _____

   _____

   _____

2. No amount of money could _____ me into betraying my country. (deduce; seduce)

   _____

   _____

   _____

3. After carefully studying the results of the experiment, Dr. Stein was able to _____ several important theories about the compound. (deduce; seduce)

   _____

   _____

   _____

4. With patience, a good teacher will _____ even the most reluctant student's desire to learn. (educe; abduct)

   _____

   _____

   _____

5. As power was handed over to the members of the new _____, the people hoped that peace would prevail. (regalia; regime)

   _____

   _____

   _____

6. Dan's daily _____ includes three well-balanced, low-fat meals. (regime; regimen)

   _____

   _____

   _____

Each question below contains a vocabulary word from this lesson. Answer each question "yes" or "no" in the space provided.

7. Is it possible to *adduce* your weight by 20 pounds by staying on a strict diet?

7. _____

8. In medieval times would you expect to find a *regnant* king in a castle?

8. _____

9. Is the military a highly *regimented* organization?

9. _____

10. Could a home be heated by forcing warmed air through an *abduct*?

10. _____

For each question you answered "no," write a sentence using the vocabulary word correctly.

_____

_____

_____

_____

_____

_____

_____

_____

_____

_____

_____

_____

Test-Taking Strategies

The Scholastic Aptitude Test (SAT) includes a section on reading comprehension. These tests ask you to read one or two selections and then answer some questions to see how well you understand what you read. The questions do not ask you simply to recall the details — they ask you to draw inferences from the information. For example, if the selection says someone mopped the sweat from his forehead, you might infer that he was hot.

Practice: Reread the selection *Peaks and Politics* on page 99. Write an X next to the statement(s) that might be inferred from this essay.

1. John D. Rockefeller was quite wealthy.

1. _____

2. The Tetons are overcrowded with tourists.

2. _____

3. Franklin D. Roosevelt was a great president.

3. _____

4. The demand for beef dropped after World War I.

4. _____

Name _____

How well do you remember the words you studied in Lessons 25 through 27? Take the following test covering the words from the last three lessons.

Part 1 Choose the Correct Meaning

Each question below includes a word in capital letters, followed by four words or phrases. Choose the word or phrase that is <u>closest</u> in meaning to the word in capital letters. Write the letter for your answer on the line provided.

Sample

| **S. FINISH** | (A) complete | (B) enjoy | S. ___**A**___ |
| | (C) destroy | (D) enlarge | |

1. REGIMENT
(A) explain carefully   (B) to put in order
(C) reject   (D) deny nutriments

1. _____

2. QUANDARY
(A) solution   (B) characteristic
(C) dilemma   (D) nervousness

2. _____

3. UNFOUNDED
(A) hidden   (B) dull
(C) remarkable   (D) not valid

3. _____

4. SUPERSEDE
(A) replace   (B) follow
(C) raise in status   (D) increase

4. _____

5. ENIGMA
(A) opponent   (B) sign of rank
(C) vigor   (D) mystery

5. _____

6. DEDUCE
(A) subtract   (B) infer
(C) postpone   (D) consider

6. _____

7. REGNANT
(A) reigning   (B) inferior
(C) democratic   (D) splendid

7. _____

8. PERPLEX
(A) explain   (B) annoy
(C) confuse   (D) deceive

8. _____

9. INEFFABLE
(A) free of errors   (B) ineffective
(C) indescribable   (D) foolish

9. _____

10. BLAZON
(A) burn   (B) display
(C) slander   (D) shatter

10. _____

11. FUTILE
(A) indestructible   (B) energetic
(C) essential   (D) ineffective

11. _____

Go on to next page. ➤

12. EDUCE   (A) bring out   (B) give up   12. _____
         (C) wipe out   (D) take advantage of

13. ABDUCT   (A) release   (B) abandon   13. _____
         (C) subdue   (D) kidnap

14. CONVOLUTED   (A) impossible   (B) complicated   14. _____
         (C) significant   (D) honored

15. RUDIMENTARY   (A) complete   (B) discourteous   15. _____
         (C) elementary   (D) customary

Part 2 Matching Words and Meanings

Match the definition in Column B with the word in Column A.
Write the letter of the correct definition on the line provided.

Column A   **Column B**

16. conundrum   a. to present as proof

17. labyrinth   b. riddle   16. _____

18. regalia   c. specialized vocabulary   17. _____

19. ascendancy   d. emblems and symbols of royalty   18. _____

20. cryptic   e. government   19. _____

21. adduce   f. maze   20. _____

22. soluble   g. mysterious   21. _____

23. lingo   h. primitive chemistry   22. _____

24. regime   i. superiority   23. _____

25. alchemy   j. able to be solved   24. _____

                                                        25. _____

Name _____

Wisdom of the Ages

If you go barefoot, don't plant thorns.

Haste makes waste.

Variety is the spice of life.

These **pithy** statements are examples of proverbs, often called the short-est art form. They use devices associated with poetry—rhythm, rhyme, and metaphor—to create vivid images that teach life's lessons. Sometimes referred to as "the wisdom of thousands, the wit of one," proverbs are
5   chunks of human experience compressed into **terse** sentences. They tend to have several layers of meaning and apply to various situations. This may explain the **ostensible** folk wisdom of "Look before you leap" and "Absence makes the heart grow fonder."

Proverbs are an **integral** part of the oral tradition of most cultures and are
10   often similar from one country to the next. They tend to follow patterns, like "Where there is X, there is Y" and "One of something is worth great amounts of something else." This latter design is **manifest** in such advice as "One good head is better than a hundred strong hands" (England), "A friend is better than a thousand silver pieces" (Greece), and "A moment
15   is worth a thousand gold pieces" (Korea).

The origins of proverbs are **disparate**; the Bible, mythology, and ancient philosophy are all sources of proverbial wisdom. While a few can proba-bly be attributed to a specific person, most were invented by ordinary peo-ple in everyday circumstances. For example, "Don't buy a pig in a
20   poke" originated hundreds of years ago in the European marketplace, where unscrupulous merchants substituted cats for pigs. A poke was a bag for carrying goods, and shoppers who thought they were buying a pig in a poke might discover too late that they had bought a cat instead. This may also account for the expression "The cat's out of the bag." Some old
25   sayings, like "An apple a day keeps the doctor away," don't seem valid any-more. Yet in spite of the passing of time, many proverbs remain quite **apt**.

Proverbs, however, can be dangerous. Poetic devices like rhythm and **ellipsis** make their lessons so condensed and powerful that they sound true. But this prepackaged wisdom is not always useful or **meritorious**. For
30   example, "Spare the rod and spoil the child" implies that physical punish-ment builds good character in children. Yet research suggests that such dis-cipline can cause children to be more **inimical** than their peers. Nevertheless, proverbs continue to be treasured heirlooms, passed from one generation to the next. You know what they say—"Old habits die hard."

Words

apt

disparate

ellipsis

inimical

integral

manifest

meritorious

ostensible

pithy

terse

Each word in this lesson's word list appears in dark type in the selection you just read. Think about how the vocabulary word is used in the selection, then write the letter for the best answer to each question.

1. Which words could best replace *pithy* in line 1?
   (A) showing a lack of judgment
   (B) forceful and brief
   (C) causing harm
   (D) characterized by repetition

   1. _____

2. Which word or words could best replace *terse* in line 5?
   (A) vigilant
   (B) irreverent
   (C) loud
   (D) brief and to the point

   2. _____

3. Which word could best replace *ostensible* in line 7?
   (A) apparent
   (B) confusing
   (C) unimaginative
   (D) uninformed

   3. _____

4. Which word or words could best replace *integral* in line 9?
   (A) ridiculous
   (B) essential for completeness
   (C) embarrassing
   (D) highly theoretical

   4. _____

5. Which word or words could best replace *manifest* in line 12?
   (A) absent
   (B) joyful
   (C) obvious
   (D) having regular cycles

   5. _____

6. Which word or words could best replace *disparate* in line 16?
   (A) different
   (B) subject to destruction
   (C) repetitive
   (D) unable to change

   6. _____

7. Which word could best replace *apt* in line 26?
   (A) allowable
   (B) unlikely
   (C) disappointing
   (D) appropriate

   7. _____

8. An *ellipsis* (line 28) can best be explained as a(n)_____.
   (A) deceptive appearance
   (B) omission of a word or phrase
   (C) downward movement
   (D) lengthy description

   8. _____

9. Which word or words could best replace *meritorious* in line 29?
   (A) deserving praise
   (B) informal
   (C) false
   (D) lacking intensity

   9. _____

10. Which word or words could best replace *inimical* in line 32?
    (A) inspiring wonder and awe
    (B) satisfied
    (C) hostile
    (D) full of meaning

    10. _____

Applying Meaning

Decide which word in parentheses best completes the sentence. Then write the sentence, adding the missing word.

1. The student received a _____ answer to his longwinded question. (disparate; terse)

   _____

   _____

   _____

2. The presence of police officers at the rock concert was _____ to direct traffic, but everyone knew there was another motive. (inimically; ostensibly)

   _____

   _____

   _____

3. The firefighter was honored at his retirement party for his _____ service to the community. (meritorious; pithy)

   _____

   _____

   _____

4. There should be a National Hostility Week to allow people to display their _____ reactions to events that have rubbed them the wrong way. (inimical; pithy)

   _____

   _____

   _____

5. Franklin D. Roosevelt _____ described December 7, 1941, as "a date which will live in infamy." (aptly; disparately)

   _____

   _____

   _____

Read each sentence below. Write "correct" on the answer line if the vocabulary word has been used correctly. Write "incorrect" on the answer line if the vocabulary word has been used incorrectly.

6. After the previous speech, which lasted almost two hours, Lincoln's two-minute address at Gettysburg was quite *pithy*.

6. _____

7. The cornered murderer warned that he was *disparate* and would stop at nothing to escape.

7. _____

8. Astronomers set up their telescopes to observe the *ellipsis* of the moon.

8. _____

9. Although many politicians wanted to ignore the problem of slavery, the issue was *manifest* each time a state applied for admission to the Union.

9. _____

10. Tests seem to be an *integral* part of every course I take in school.

10. _____

For each word used incorrectly, write a sentence using the word properly.

_____

_____

_____

_____

_____

_____

_____

_____

_____

_____

_____

_____

_____

Mastering Meaning

Try creating your own proverb. You might use the pattern "One . . . is worth a thousand . . . ." Write an explanation of its meaning, using some of the words you studied in this lesson.

Name _____

"How much do you want?" *"How much* does it cost?" *"How much* is left?" *"How much* do you need?"* Many of the questions that confront us daily are questions of amount or quantity. In this lesson, you will learn ten words associated with these questions.

Unlocking Meaning

A vocabulary word appears in italics in each sentence or short passage below. Think about how the word is used in the passage. Then write a definition for the vocabulary word. Compare your definition with the definition on the flash card.

Words
apportion
curtail
discernible
exorbitant
imperceptible
infinitesimal
lavish
modicum
parity
prodigious

1. In an interview with a local television reporter, Mr. Margolis said he plans to *apportion* the money he won in the lottery among his four grandchildren. He wants each one to be able to afford a college education.

   _____

   _____

   _____

2. During a long heat wave, people often use an excessive amount of electricity. To prevent a major power outage, representatives of public utilities sometimes ask people to *curtail* their use of electricity during hot weather.

   _____

   _____

   _____

3. The lights of approaching cars were barely *discernible* in the fog. Such poor visibility can be quite hazardous.

   _____

   _____

   _____

4. For weeks after the hurricane, drinking water was quite scarce. During that time, some unscrupulous merchants sold bottled water at *exorbitant* prices.

   _____

   _____

   _____

5. According to seismographic readings, a minor earthquake occurred around noon today. But because the earth's movement was almost *imperceptible*, many people were unaware of the quake until they watched the evening news.

_____

_____

_____

6. Ensuring that the space probe would pass close to Pluto required very exact navigational calculations. Even an *infinitesimal* error could send the satellite hundreds of miles off its course.

_____

_____

_____

7. Estella was embarrassed by the *lavish* praise she received for rescuing the child from the burning car. She didn't believe that she deserved so much attention for doing what anyone in that situation would have done.

_____

_____

_____

8. "If you had even a *modicum* of pride, you wouldn't wear old jeans with holes in the knees," my grandmother scolded.

_____

_____

_____

9. The senators decided to tax the cheaply produced imports in order to create price *parity* with items produced in this country. If imported goods cost the same as domestic goods, they reasoned, most people would buy the American product.

_____

_____

_____

10. After sixteen snowstorms in twelve weeks, a *prodigious* amount of snow had accumulated in our area. On our street an eight-foot snow bank became a winter playground for the children.

_____

_____

_____

Applying Meaning

Each question below contains at least one vocabulary word from this lesson. Answer each question "yes" or "no" in the space provided.

1. Are slight changes in temperature often *imperceptible*?

1. _____

2. Would a smart shopper be a frequent customer at a store that charges *exorbitant* prices?

2. _____

3. Would someone with a *prodigious* appetite eat *infinitesimal* amounts of food?

3. _____

4. Would it be wise for someone who has lost his or her job to *curtail* all unnecessary spending?

4. _____

5. Is someone who has a *modicum* of success as an artist likely to live in a *lavishly* furnished home?

5. _____

6. Would a reasonable employer attempt to provide *parity* in the salaries of workers performing similar work?

6. _____

For each question you answered "no," write a sentence using the vocabulary word(s) correctly.

_____

_____

_____

_____

_____

_____

_____

_____

_____

_____

Follow the directions below to write a sentence using a vocabulary word.

7. Describe a historic landmark on a foggy day. Use any form of the word *discernible*.

_____

_____

_____

8. Use any form of the word *apportion* in a sentence about distributing a limited supply of tickets for a popular event.

_____

_____

_____

9. Tell about an experience you or someone you know had shopping. Use any form of the word *exorbitant*.

_____

_____

_____

10. Describe someone who is extremely gifted. Use any form of the word *prodigious*.

_____

_____

_____

Bonus Word

titan

According to Greek mythology, the Titans were remarkably strong giants who ruled the universe. They were eventually overthrown by the family of Zeus. Nowadays a person of remarkable strength or achievement is sometimes referred to as a titan. For example, there are titans of industry, titans of literature, and titans of sport. A huge luxury ocean liner that was considered unsinkable was named the *Titanic.* When it sank on its maiden voyage in 1912, its name took on an especially ironic twist.

Write a Report: Choose someone you consider a titan in a particular field. Write a report explaining why you chose this person. Use some of the words you studied in this lesson.

Name _____

The Latin *-leuk-*, meaning "light" or "brightness," is the source of our roots *-luc-* and *-lumin-*. The Greek word *logos*, meaning "speech," "reason" or "word" gives us the common root *-log-*. Each of the vocabulary words in this lesson has one of these roots.

Root	Meaning	English Word
-luc-	light, brightness	lucid
-lumin-		luminary
-log-	speech, word, reason	monologue

Unlocking Meaning

Read the sentences or short passages below. Write the letter for the correct definition of the italicized vocabulary word.

The instructor used an *analogy* to explain how a computer works. He asked us to think of the computer's memory as a huge file cabinet that is divided into drawers, files, and individual documents.

1. (A) humorous story
   (B) confusing arrangement
   (C) comparison of two dissimilar things
   (D) ancient system of measurement

Many of his supporters misunderstood the candidate's remark. As a result, he held a press conference and attempted to *elucidate* his position.

2. (A) hide
   (B) erase
   (C) find
   (D) clarify

In spite of the confusion, Sharon was able to give investigators a *lucid* account of what had happened when the train collided with the truck.

3. (A) clear
   (B) foggy
   (C) wild and hysterical
   (D) confused

As a *luminary* in the field of cancer treatment, Dr. Carvell is respected and sought after, not only in the United States but all over the world.

4. (A) an unknown
   (B) a fake or fraud
   (C) a person of brilliant achievement
   (D) someone who travels extensively

Words

analogy

elucidate

logistics

lucid

luminary

monologue

neologism

relucent

tautology

translucent

1.

2.

3. _____

4.

The PTA meeting was supposed to be in the form of a debate, but it turned into a *monologue* when Ms. Skinner spoke for more than an hour without allowing questions or rebuttal.

5. (A) long speech given by one person
   (B) series of questions for which there are no answers
   (C) conversation between two or more people
   (D) one-line speech

5. _____

The first time someone called me an audiophile I was not sure whether I had been insulted or complimented. Since then I have learned that this *neologism* from the fifties simply means someone who is passionate about stereos and sound reproduction.

6. (A) slanderous remark
   (B) overused word or expression
   (C) humorous story
   (D) newly invented word or expression

6. _____

After Abe polished the chrome on his old car, the bumper was so *relucent* that you almost needed sunglasses to look at it.

7. (A) invisible
   (B) shiny
   (C) worn and dull
   (D) damaged

7. _____

The *logistics* involved in the Normandy landing were remarkable. The movement of thousands of soldiers, equipment, and supplies, as well as the food, ammunition, and medical support essential to maintain them on shore had to be carefully coordinated.

8. (A) lengthy discussion
   (B) enjoyment
   (C) handling of the details of an operation
   (D) musical entertainment

8. _____

The speaker kept referring to "modern teenagers in today's contemporary society." By eliminating this *tautology* alone, she could have cut the length of the speech in half.

9. (A) unnecessary repetition
   (B) bad grammar
   (C) punctuation
   (D) inspirational message

9. _____

Through the *translucent* curtains, we could see two people moving inside the house, but we couldn't determine if they were men or women.

10. (A) allowing no light to enter
    (B) admitting light but blocking a clear view
    (C) expensive
    (D) homemade

10. _____

Name _____

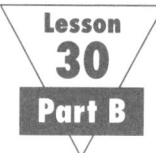
Applying Meaning

Decide which word in parentheses best completes the sentence. Then write the sentence, adding the missing word.

1. Moving the entire office to a new building without disrupting business will require great _____ planning. (logistical; translucent)

   _____

   _____

   _____

2. Because of the _____ quality of frosted glass, it is often used in places where people want both light and privacy. (relucent; translucent)

   _____

   _____

   _____

3. The actor's understudy had trouble memorizing the _____ in the last act of the play. (monologue; neologism)

   _____

   _____

   _____

4. At the end of the lecture, several students asked the teacher to _____ her point about the origins of socialism. (analogy; elucidate)

   _____

   _____

   _____

5. Lincoln used the _____ that the Union, like a house divided, could not survive "half slave and half free." (analogy; tautology)

   _____

   _____

   _____

6. Thanks to Fareed's _____ explanation of the problem, we were able to repair the engine in time for the trip. (concurrent; lucid)

   _____

   _____

   _____

7. If the _____ had been eliminated from the essay, it would have been more concise and much more interesting. (luminaries; tautologies)

_____

_____

_____

8. We thought there would be sports celebrities at the banquet, but there wasn't a single _____ in sight all evening. (luminary; translucent)

_____

_____

_____

Follow the directions below to write a sentence using a vocabulary word.

9. Use any form of the word *relucent* to describe the surface of an object.

_____

_____

_____

10. Use *neologism* in a sentence about a word that has become popular.

_____

_____

_____

Cultural Literacy Note

"To be, or not to be: that is the question"

The well-known words "To be, or not to be" begin one of the most famous monologues in all of literature. The words are spoken by the title character in Shakespeare's tragedy *Hamlet*. In this monologue, Hamlet wonders aloud about suicide. This monologue has given the language many familiar expressions, such as "the slings and arrows of outrageous fortune" and "conscience does make cowards of us all."

Cooperative Learning: Working with a partner, get a copy of Hamlet's complete monologue and rewrite it, using more familiar language. Read your version and Shakespeare's version to the class and discuss which version is more lucid and which is more powerful.

Lessons 28-30

Name _____

How well do you remember the words you studied in Lessons 28 through 30? Take the following test covering the words from the last three lessons.

Part 1 Antonyms

Each question below includes a word in capital letters, followed by four words or phrases. Choose the word or phrase that is most nearly <u>opposite</u> in meaning to the word in capital letters. Consider all choices before deciding on your answer. Write the letter for your answer on the line provided.

Sample

S. HIGH	(A) cold	(B) simple	**S.** ____**C**____
	(C) low	(D) foolish	

1. PARITY   (A) fairness   (B) inequality   1. _____
                 (C) uniformity   (D) distortion

2. ELUCIDATE   (A) imprison   (B) attract   2. _____
                 (C) explain   (D) confuse

3. PITHY   (A) pitiless   (B) vague   3. _____
                 (C) unusual   (D) clever

4. RELUCENT   (A) dull   (B) cautious   4. _____
                 (C) eager   (D) persistent

5. CURTAIL   (A) twist   (B) relieve   5. _____
                 (C) prolong   (D) shorten

6. APT   (A) exceptional   (B) healthy   6. _____
                 (C) lazy   (D) inappropriate

7. IMPERCEPTIBLE   (A) invisible   (B) obvious   7. _____
                 (C) fragile   (D) accomplishment

8. PRODIGIOUS   (A) small   (B) conspicuous   8. _____
                 (C) enormous   (D) shy

9. DISPARATE   (A) energetic   (B) happy   9. _____
                 (C) same   (D) desperate

10. LUCID   (A) reasonable   (B) understandable   10. _____
                 (C) disloyal   (D) unclear

Go on to next page. ➤

11. MODICUM   (A) example   (B) method   11. _____
                    (C) large amount   (D) limitation

12. INTEGRAL   (A) unnecessary   (B) clearly marked   12. _____
                    (C) impossible   (D) ridiculous

13. OSTENSIBLE   (A) hidden   (B) quiet   13. _____
                    (C) dangerous   (D) sturdy

14. MERITORIOUS   (A) famous   (B) worthless   14. _____
                    (C) disorganized   (D) honorable

15. DISCERNIBLE   (A) careful   (B) unconcerned   15. _____
                    (C) tasty   (D) invisible

Part 2 Matching Words and Meanings

Match the definition in Column B with the word in Column A.
Write the letter of the correct definition on the line provided.

Column A	Column B	
16. apportion	a. brief and to the point	16. _____
17. inimical	b. extravagant	17. _____
18. luminary	c. distribute according to a plan	18. _____
19. lavish	d. obvious	19. _____
20. tautology	e. excessive	20. _____
21. exorbitant	f. hostile	21. _____
22. terse	g. type of comparison	22. _____
23. analogy	h. long speech	23. _____
24. monologue	i. needless repetition	24. _____
25. manifest	j. celebrity	25. _____

Name _____

The Moche of Ancient Peru

On a banner, **meticulously wrought** tiny golden human figures wear bracelets of minuscule turquoise beads, gilded copper chestpieces, and nose ornaments made of sheet gold. Seabirds, crayfish, land snails, and spiders march across mosaics of gold and semiprecious stones and shells.

5   These are but a few examples of the **grandiose** treasure buried nearly 2,000 years ago by the Moche, a pre-Incan people who inhabited 250 miles of Peru's coast. The Moche never developed a written language; they told their story in finely crafted precious metals and exceptional pottery.

During the first century A.D., when the Roman Empire was approaching

10 its height, the Moche were creating one of the most remarkable civilizations of the ancient world. To sustain this **florescent** culture, they needed a diverse, thriving, and well-organized economy. They used rivers to create a network of irrigation canals that watered thousands of acres in **arid** coastal valleys, producing crops of corn, beans, avocados, squash, chili

15 peppers, and peanuts. They domesticated ducks, llamas, and guinea pigs and harvested fish, shrimp, and crabs from the ocean.

The Moche excelled not only in art but also in technology. They built **truncated** pyramids that rose up to 135 feet and sprawled over ten acres. They were the first people in South America to produce pottery from

20 molds, making a wide range of ceramics available to all. Centuries before the invention of electroplating, Moche metalsmiths devised a method that bound thin layers of gold and silver to copper. They perfected stamps to decorate pots and vessels with elaborate **iconography** that portrayed scenes from daily life. Moche sculptors were **sublimely** talented at render-

25 ing subtle facial features. Although later civilizations in the area produced impressive ceramics and metals, they never achieved the artistic genius of the Moche.

By 800 A.D. Moche civilization had disappeared. Earthquakes and relentless droughts may have undermined the economic foundation of the civ-

30 ilization, but there were probably other forces at work as well. The art had lost many of the characteristics of the glory days. The artists even made mistakes, showing people in inappropriate costume. By the time the Spaniards arrived in the early sixteenth century, **sporadic deluges** from the destructive weather of El Niño had over the years eroded the mud-

35 brick pyramids and palaces. Exactly what or who brought an end to the majesty of the Moche remains as much a mystery as the fall of their contemporaries, the Maya. Not even the Moche's gold, silver, and ceramic creations can divulge that secret.

Words
arid
deluge
florescent
grandiose
iconography
meticulous
sporadic
sublime
truncate
wrought

Each word in this lesson's word list appears in dark type in the selection you just read. Think about how the vocabulary word is used in the selection, then write the letter for the best answer to each question.

1. Which word or words could best replace *meticulously* in line 1?
   (A) carefully and precisely   (B) intellectually
   (C) overwhelmingly   (D) foolishly

   1. _____

2. Which word or words could best replace *wrought* in line 1?
   (A) relieved of obligation   (B) supplied to the fullest extent
   (C) established   (D) created or formed

   2. _____

3. Which word or words could best replace *grandiose* in line 5?
   (A) passing away quickly   (B) boldly stylish
   (C) impressive   (D) showing little preparation

   3. _____

4. Which word or words could best replace *florescent* in line 11?
   (A) harmless   (B) blossoming
   (C) immoral   (D) peculiar

   4. _____

5. Which word or words could best replace *arid* in line 13?
   (A) readily accessible   (B) easily irritated
   (C) clumsy   (D) dry and barren

   5. _____

6. Something that is *truncated* (line 18) can best be explained as _____.
   (A) grossly wicked   (B) dense
   (C) shortened as if a part   (D) lopsided
       were cut off

   6. _____

7. *Iconography* (line 23) can best be explained as the _____.
   (A) pictorial illustration of a subject
   (B) simultaneous playing of one melody by several instruments
   (C) extraction of different substances from precious metals
   (D) science of measuring time

   7. _____

8. Which word could best replace *sublimely* in line 24?
   (A) moderately   (B) supremely
   (C) rebelliously   (D) deliberately

   8. _____

9. Which word or words could best replace *sporadic* in line 33?
   (A) richly interesting   (B) constant
   (C) unhurried   (D) occurring irregularly

   9. _____

10. *Deluges* (line 33) can best be explained as _____.
    (A) great floods   (B) dominant themes
    (C) vital parts   (D) ancient precious stones

    10. _____

Applying Meaning

Decide which vocabulary word in parentheses best completes the sentence. Then write the sentence, adding the missing word.

1. "Clip art" or "dingbats" allow computer users to create letters or other documents entirely from _____. (iconography; florescence)

   _____

   _____

   _____

2. In the original movie version of "Sunset Boulevard," Gloria Swanson was _____ as the faded movie queen Norma Desmond. (arid; sublime)

   _____

   _____

   _____

3. Jack Kerouac's *On the Road* was a tribute to the _____ of the Beat Generation of the 1950s. (florescence; iconography)

   _____

   _____

   _____

4. During the 1980s, the introduction of cable television precipitated a _____ of news, sports, and music programs. (deluge; truncation)

   _____

   _____

   _____

5. Even the name Death Valley suggests a(n) _____, unfriendly environment. (arid; grandiose)

   _____

   _____

   _____

6. Mesas are clifflike formations whose tops have been _____ by centuries of erosion. (truncated; wrought)

   _____

   _____

   _____

7. Bill's claim that he can finish high school in three years and graduate first in his class is just a _____ boast. (grandiose; meticulous)

_____

_____

_____

8. Before any planting takes place, landscape architects make _____ drawings of how the planted area will look. (meticulous; sporadic)

_____

_____

_____

9. Bali silversmiths excel in finely _____ projections that decorate the surface of jewelry. (deluged; wrought)

_____

_____

_____

10. The weather forecast for yesterday called for _____ showers in our area. (sublime; sporadic)

_____

_____

_____

Mastering Meaning

Select an ancient civilization, such as the Incan, Mayan, or Minoan, and go to the library to research it. Then write a brief report in which you discuss one of its unique characteristics or mysteries or describe some of the artifacts typical of the culture. Use some of the words you studied in this lesson.

Lesson
32
Part A

Name _____

Everyone is good at something. You may be a great cook or a math genius, while a friend possesses exceptional artistic ability. English has a number of words for describing abilities and interests. In this lesson, you will learn ten of them.

Unlocking Meaning

Words

acuity

adept

aesthete

connoisseur

deft

finesse

perspicacious

precocious

savant

virtuoso

Read the sentences or short passages below. Write the letter for the correct definition of the italicized vocabulary word.

Assistant district attorney Barbara Yu's mental *acuity* is a valuable asset in the courtroom. She analyzes evidence quickly and knows exactly which questions to ask of a witness.

1. (A) deficiency
   (B) sharpness
   (C) dependence on others
   (D) lack of restraint

When Mr. Gardner saw how *adept* a swimmer Beatrice was, he asked her to teach one of the intermediate swimming classes.

2. (A) highly skilled
   (B) unusual
   (C) argumentative
   (D) poorly trained

Rolando is quite the *aesthete*. He says that nothing makes him happier than spending hours at the art museum looking at paintings and daydreaming. He wants to lead tours at the museum so he can share his love of art with others.

1. _____

3. (A) a museum security guard
   (B) someone with little regard for art
   (C) someone with exceptional athletic ability
   (D) someone with great sensitivity to beauty

2. _____

The magazine included an article by a well-known *connoisseur* of fine wines. His books on the subject are considered required reading for all French chefs.

3. _____

4. (A) accomplished imitator
   (B) person who lacks proper training
   (C) expert in matters of art and good taste
   (D) artist with a large following

4. _____

The Japanese waiter chopped the vegetables and shrimp for our meal with amazing speed and precision, his knives seemingly flying through the air. Such *deft* handling of sharp knives must take months of training.

5. (A) awkward
   (B) entertaining
   (C) deceptive
   (D) skillful and quick

5. _____

Changing a damaged sail in the middle of a race requires great *finesse* and remarkable teamwork. The torn sail must be lowered and moved out of the way and the other sail raised with little or no loss of speed.

6. (A) skillful handling
   (B) knowledge of the weather
   (C) enjoyment
   (D) disregard for one's personal safety

6. _____

Although everyone else was baffled by the puzzling clues found at the crime scene, Detective McCarthy knew immediately what had happened. She is too *perspicacious* to be outsmarted by any criminal.

7. (A) confused
   (B) keenly intelligent; clever
   (C) likely to tire quickly
   (D) quick to jump to conclusions

7. _____

I had spent days reading the manual and studying the parts, but it took Ms. Lobocek's *precocious* ten-year-old daughter only five minutes to fix my malfunctioning computer.

8. (A) unable to speak
   (B) rude and offensive
   (C) trustworthy
   (D) showing early mental development

8. _____

Mr. Raciti has become quite a *savant*. He spends every summer vacation taking graduate-level courses and doing research.

9. (A) aimless wanderer
   (B) elderly celebrity
   (C) person of learning
   (D) geography student

9. _____

At the age of fifteen, George was already more accomplished than his piano teacher. Everyone who heard him play was sure that he would become a great *virtuoso*.

10. (A) musician of exceptional skill
    (B) artist living overseas
    (C) person possessing great virtue and morality
    (D) unemployed musician

10. _____

Applying Meaning

Follow the directions below to write a sentence using a vocabulary word.

1. Use the word *savant* in a sentence about a student in a mathematics class.

   _____

   _____

   _____

2. Describe a detective's work on a difficult case. Use any form of the word *acuity*.

   _____

   _____

   _____

3. Describe a young child. Use the word *precocious*.

   _____

   _____

   _____

4. Write a sentence about someone you know who does something particularly well. Use any form of the word *adept*.

   _____

   _____

   _____

5. Use any form of the word *deft* to describe how a difficult task was accomplished.

   _____

   _____

   _____

6. Use any form of the word *virtuoso* in a sentence about a performance you attended or would like to attend.

   _____

   _____

   _____

Each question below contains a vocabulary word from this lesson. Answer each question "yes" or "no" in the space provided.

7. Does performing in a ballet require a high degree of *finesse*?

7. _____

8. Would a football coach want his best *aesthetes* in the game for an important play?

8. _____

9. Is a *connoisseur* a type of prehistoric creature?

9. _____

10. Would it be helpful to have a *perspicacious* commander planning a military action?

10. _____

For each question you answered "no," write a sentence using the vocabulary word correctly.

_____

_____

_____

_____

_____

_____

_____

_____

_____

_____

Bonus Word

dilettante

Many English words having to do with the arts come from Italian. One such word is *dilettante*, which means "lover of the arts." However, like the word *aesthete*, it is often used in a negative sense to mean someone who pretends to be cultured, but in reality has only a superficial or amateurish knowledge of art.

Use the Dictionary: Look up the definitions of these words: *dabbler, neophyte, trifler,* and *tyro*. Write a brief character sketch of an imaginary person who would fit each definition.

Name _____

The Latin word *stare,* which means "to stand," usually appears in English words as the root *-sta-* or *-stit-*. The Latin word *stringere,* which means "to draw tight" or "to bind," usually appears in English words as the root *-strin-*. It can also be spelled *-stra-* and *-stric-*. Each vocabulary word in this lesson has one of these roots.

Root	Meaning	English Word
-sta-	to stand	statute
-stit-		destitute
-strin-	to draw tight,	stringent
-stra-	to bind	constrain
-stric-		constrict

Unlocking Meaning

A vocabulary word appears in italics in each sentence or short passage below. Find the root in the vocabulary word and think about how the word is used in the passage. Then write a definition for the vocabulary word. Compare your definition with the definition on the flash card.

1. The tragic death of the infant was an *astringent* reminder that babies and toddlers must be securely strapped into their car seats.

   _____

   _____

   _____

2. The prosecution's case against the defendant was purely *circumstantial.* While the defendant could not prove he was out of town at the time of the crime, and he had a well-known dislike for the victim, there was no other evidence to connect him to the assault.

   _____

   _____

   _____

3. The senator promised her *constituency* that she would fight in Congress for lower taxes and a tough anticrime bill. "After all," she added, "that is why you elected me to this office."

   _____

   _____

   _____

Words

astringent

circumstantial

constituency

constrain

constrict

destitute

restitution

stature

statute

stringent

4. After hearing the proposal to limit access to the town beach, Lina felt *constrained* to speak out. The beaches belong to everyone, she said.

_____

_____

_____

5. Sabu forgot that he had *constricted* his wrist with the rubber band. After an hour, it had nearly stopped the flow of blood to his hand.

_____

_____

_____

6. Many *destitute* people living on the streets of our cities once had jobs, homes, and enough money to pay their bills.

_____

_____

_____

7. The students should make *restitution* for the damage to the computer they vandalized. After all, it will cost nearly $500 to repair.

_____

_____

_____

8. Oscar is a superb athlete in many ways. However, until his team wins the championship, he will never achieve the *stature* of a superstar.

_____

_____

_____

9. Julian said that Boston still has a *statute* that allows residents of Beacon Hill to graze their cows on Boston Common.

_____

_____

_____

10. Danielle withdrew her application for membership in the country club when she learned about its *stringent* regulations. She had no intention of dressing in formal attire just to eat in the dining room.

_____

_____

_____

Applying Meaning

Read each sentence or short passage below. Write "correct" on the answer line if the vocabulary word has been used correctly. Write "incorrect" on the answer line if the vocabulary word has been used incorrectly.

1. We stopped in front of the *statute* of Paul Revere to read the inscription on the base.

2. The musician believed that she was *destitute* to be a concert pianist.

3. The judge ordered the thief to make *restitution* to the shopkeeper.

4. The monastery required anyone seeking admission to abide by *stringent* rules on diet, prayer, and work.

5. Ms. Mahoney's *stature* rose in the eyes of her students when she agreed to meet with them on Saturday to review for the test.

6. After waiting for weeks for an answer to my question, I did not feel *constrained* to return her urgent call.

7. This pamphlet will *constrict* you on how to apply for a driver's license.

8. In geometry class we studied the rules for finding the area of *circumstantial* objects.

1. _____

2. _____

3. _____

4. _____

5. _____

6. _____

7. _____

8. _____

For each word used incorrectly, write a sentence using the word properly.

_____
_____
_____
_____
_____
_____
_____
_____
_____
_____
_____
_____
_____
_____
_____

Decide which word in parentheses best completes the sentence. Then write the sentence, adding the missing word.

9. The man we saw coming out of the bank had blue eyes and light brown hair, and was of medium _____. (constituency; stature)

_____

_____

_____

10. The meeting seemed to be going smoothly until one board member made several _____ remarks about the chairperson's family problems. (astringent; circumstantial)

_____

_____

_____

11. The speaker reminded everyone that people who are _____ are not necessarily lazy. (circumstantial; destitute)

_____

_____

_____

12. The state representative voted according to the wishes of his _____. (constituency; statute)

_____

_____

_____

Bonus Words

restless   restive

Similar in appearance and *general* meaning, the words *restless* and *restive* are sometimes mistakenly thought to be synonyms. If someone is restless, he or she might be unable to sit still. He or she is literally "without rest." However, someone who is *restive* has become impatient because of some outside delay or restriction. Students might grow restive if the school year continued through July.

Write a Series of Sentences: Write at least three sentences using the word *restless* and three using the word *restive* to demonstrate the difference in the meaning of the two words.

Name _____

How well do you remember the words you studied in Lessons 31 through 33? Take the following test covering the words from the last three lessons.

Part 1 Choose the Correct Meaning

Each question below includes a word in capital letters, followed by four words or phrases. Choose the word or phrase that is <u>closest</u> in meaning to the word in capital letters. Write the letter for your answer on the line provided.

Sample

S. FINISH	(A) enjoy	(B) complete	**S.** _____ **B**
	(C) destroy	(D) enlarge	

1. ARID
(A) exceptional   (B) dry
(C) overwhelmed   (D) educated

1. _____

2. PRECOCIOUS
(A) precious   (B) easily angered
(C) coming later   (D) advanced

2. _____

3. ADEPT
(A) skilled   (B) concerned
(C) adjust   (D) without feelings

3. _____

4. STATURE
(A) law   (B) type of memorial
(C) status   (D) innocent victim

4. _____

5. VIRTUOSO
(A) skillful performer   (B) moral leader
(C) religious person   (D) simple machine

5. _____

6. TRUNCATE
(A) insult   (B) eliminate
(C) cultivate   (D) cut off

6. _____

7. GRANDIOSE
(A) diseased   (B) magnificent
(C) grainy   (D) wordy

7. _____

8. SPORADIC
(A) carefully crafted   (B) irregular
(C) dangerous   (D) sickly

8. _____

9. ASTRINGENT
(A) scholarly   (B) stingy
(C) harsh   (D) allowable

9. _____

10. METICULOUS
(A) solvent   (B) expressive
(C) honorable   (D) exact

10. _____

Go on to next page. ➤

11. RESTITUTION   (A) organization   (B) reimbursement   11. _____
                      (C) punishment   (D) remainder

12. CIRCUMSTANTIAL   (A) incidental   (B) geometric   12. _____
                      (C) ordinary   (D) convincing

13. DEFT   (A) clumsy   (B) senseless   13. _____
                      (C) skillful   (D) officially approved

14. FINESSE   (A) aloof attitude   (B) expensive   14. _____
                                          decorations
                      (C) final action   (D) skillful handling

15. WROUGHT   (A) flawed   (B) crafted   15. _____
                      (C) saddened   (D) thoughtful

Part 2 Matching Words and Meanings

Match the definition in Column B with the word in Column A.
Write the letter of the correct definition on the line provided.

Column A	Column B	
16. deluge	a. blossoming	16. _____
17. acuity	b. poor	17. _____
18. constrain	c. supreme	18. _____
19. constituency	d. keenness	19. _____
20. savant	e. group of voters	20. _____
21. sublime	f. someone who appreciates beauty	21. _____
22. destitute	g. huge flood	22. _____
23. florescent	h. law	23. _____
24. aesthete	i. learned person	24. _____
25. statute	j. compel	25. _____

Name _____

An Uncommon Common Liquid

The search for a universal solvent has puzzled scientists and inspired science fiction writers for generations. A magical liquid that can dissolve all known substances will probably never be found or created. And, as an old joke goes, the chemist who invents it will have a difficult time finding a container to hold it! In any event, such nearly mythical topics are seldom **broached** in **cerebral** scientific discussions.

Even though there is little scientific interest in finding a universal solvent, we have something very close to such a solvent all around us. It is the most plentiful and commonplace of all liquids — water. **Rivulets** of this colorless, odorless liquid have cut canyons in the earth. Water's actions annually **erode** thousands of acres of land, dissolving and redistributing vital topsoil.

For all its power, however, water is a deceptively simple compound. Each molecule of water consists of two atoms of hydrogen and one atom of oxygen. Scientific studies have **ascertained** that the hydrogen atoms are positioned on roughly the same side of the oxygen atom. This **configuration** gives water a very interesting **property**. Because the positive hydrogen atoms are on one side of the molecule and the negative oxygen atom is on the other, water molecules tend to **adhere** to one another. You can see evidence of this tendency if you place a drop of water on a smooth, flat surface. If you look closely you will see that it does not spread out. Instead it appears as a slightly flattened mound held together by a tight "skin." This skin, sometimes called surface tension, also exists on large bodies of water, such as lakes and ponds. Have you ever seen an insect walk across the surface of a pond? It can do that because the tension on the surface of the water is strong enough to support it.

While surface tension serves the spider well, it can pose a problem for us. Because water tends to stick to itself, it does not readily enter the tiny **recesses** found in the fibers of fabrics. Soaps and detergents are needed to break down the surface tension, allowing the molecules of water to penetrate the tight spaces between the threads in your clothes.

Water possesses another most unusual characteristic. It is one of a very few substances that exists as a solid, a liquid, and a gas within normal temperature ranges. You see it as a solid in the form of ice and snow, as a liquid when it comes from the tap, and as a gas in the form of steam when you cook. This quality of water is of no small importance. The snow that falls in the mountains, where the air is **rarefied**, melts into water that runs into streams and rivers. Eventually the water evaporates into a gas that condenses back into snow or rain, and the cycle continues. This constant recycling of the Earth's water supply is essential to all life. Although water may not be a universal solvent, we depend on its unusual properties every day.

5

10

15

20

25

30

35

40

Words
adhere
ascertain
broach
cerebral
configuration
erode
property
rarefied
recesses
rivulet

Each word in this lesson's word list appears in dark type in the selection you just read. Think about how the vocabulary word is used in the selection, then write the letter for the best answer to each question.

1. Which word or words could best replace *broached* in line 5?
   (A) brought up for discussion   (B) ridiculed
   (C) dismissed casually   (D) completely condemned

   1. _____

2. A *cerebral* discussion (line 6) is best described as ____.
   (A) magical   (B) intellectual
   (C) poetic   (D) humorous

   2. _____

3. A *rivulet* (line 9) can best be described as a ____.
   (A) metal tank   (B) piece of jewelry
   (C) small brook or stream   (D) type of poetry

   3. _____

4. Which word or words could best replace *erode* in line 10?
   (A) wear away   (B) fertilize
   (C) create   (D) enrich

   4. _____

5. If something is *ascertained* (line 14), it is ____.
   (A) hidden   (B) released
   (C) dissolved in a strong   (D) learned with certainty
       chemical

   5. _____

6. Which word or words could best replace *configuration* in line 15?
   (A) description   (B) arrangement of parts or
                          elements
   (C) argument   (D) rapid motion

   6. _____

7. In line 16, the word *property* means ____.
   (A) history   (B) explanation
   (C) container   (D) characteristic

   7. _____

8. Which word could best replace *adhere* in line 18?
   (A) cling   (B) pass
   (C) look   (D) disappear

   8. _____

9. Which word or words could best replace *recesses* in line 28?
   (A) imperfections   (B) insects
   (C) labels   (D) small holes

   9. _____

10. Which word or words could best replace *rarefied* in line 36?
    (A) thinned out   (B) expensive
    (C) easily destroyed (D) insignificant

    10. _____

Applying Meaning

Follow the directions below to write a sentence using a vocabulary word.

1. Describe a discussion you witnessed or engaged in. Use any form of the word *broach* in your description.

_____

_____

_____

2. Use any form of the word *adhere* in a sentence about a crafts project.

_____

_____

_____

3. Describe a scene after a thunderstorm. Use any form of the word *rivulet*.

_____

_____

_____

4. Describe a formation of clouds or stars. Use any form of the word *configuration*.

_____

_____

_____

5. Use any form of the word *property* to describe an unusual rock you might find.

_____

_____

_____

6. Describe someone's actions or behavior. Use the word *cerebral*.

_____

_____

_____

Decide which word in parentheses best completes the sentence. Then write the sentence, adding the missing word.

7. Before accusing anyone of stealing the final examination questions, the principal needed to _____ all the facts about their disappearance. (adhere; ascertain)

_____

_____

_____

8. Conversation among the physics professors can become quite _____ . (eroded; rarefied)

_____

_____

_____

9. Our guide led us to some of the most remote _____ of the cave. (properties; recesses)

_____

_____

_____

10. Little by little the salt water and the force of the tides will _____ the wooden piers. (erode; rarefy)

_____

_____

_____

Mastering Meaning

Because of the central role water plays in our lives, it is often used in poetry as a means of describing some aspect of the human condition. Read the following lines from the *Rubáiyát of Omar Khayyám* as translated by Edward FitzGerald. Write a brief explanation of their meaning. Use some words you studied in this lesson.

And this was all the Harvest that I reap'd —
"I came like Water, and like Wind I go."

Name _____

Sometimes no matter how thoroughly you plan, things just do not work out the way you had hoped. At other times, for no apparent reason, things just seem to go your way. In this lesson you will learn ten words whose meanings have something to do with luck or chance.

Unlocking Meaning

Read the sentences or short passages below. Write the letter for the correct definition of the italicized vocabulary word.

We were completely lost. The decision to turn left at the intersection was completely *arbitrary*. We might just as easily have decided to turn right.

1. (A) not guided by reason or principle
    (B) precisely calculated
    (C) hotly debated
    (D) deeply religious

First our flight was delayed. Then the hotel could not find our reservations. Finally we ducked into another hotel to escape the rain. Through this *concatenation* of events, we ended up staying in the same room in the same hotel as we did last year.

2. (A) enjoyment
    (B) connected series
    (C) simplicity
    (D) careful plan

If Kim wanted the surprise party for her parents to be successful, she would need to think of some *contrivance* to get them out of the house while the guests arrived.

3. (A) four-wheeled vehicle
    (B) criminal behavior
    (C) annoying sounds
    (D) plot; trick

There was a sense of *fatalism* at the election-eve party. Few supporters really felt that their candidate could win, but at that point there was nothing more that could be done.

4. (A) joy and high spirits
    (B) resigned acceptance
    (C) disbelief
    (D) violent rebellion

Words
arbitrary
concatenation
contrivance
fatalism
fortuitous
predisposed
providential
serendipity
spontaneous
vagary

1. _____

2. _____

3. _____

4. _____

The flat tire turned out to be a *fortuitous* event. The state police officer who stopped to help us turned out to be an old friend we had been trying to locate.

5. (A) tragic

    (B) ridiculous

    (C) fortunate

    (D) illegal

5. _____

Having heard so many jokes about New Jersey, Kara was *predisposed* to find living there quite miserable. However, she was pleasantly surprised to find her new neighborhood very clean and friendly.

6. (A) inclined toward something in advance

    (B) excited

    (C) uninformed

    (D) angrily rejected

6. _____

Just as the rescue plane was about to give up the search, a *providential* break in the clouds allowed the pilot to spot the stranded hikers.

7. (A) unfortunate

    (B) carefully planned

    (C) colorful

    (D) lucky

7. _____

A successful inventor needs a little *serendipity*. So often people make important discoveries accidentally when they are searching for something else.

8. (A) scientific research

    (B) friendly advice

    (C) ability to find good things by accident

    (D) miscalculation

8. _____

When General Grant checked into the Willard Hotel, people seated in the lobby recognized him as the new commander of the Army of the Potomac and broke into *spontaneous* applause.

9. (A) carefully planned

    (B) unrehearsed

    (C) hostile

    (D) inappropriate

9. _____

The *vagaries* of politics are enough to baffle even experienced candidates. One day you are leading in the polls, and the next day you are out of the race.

10. (A) whims

    (B) certainties

    (C) rewards

    (D) predictability

10. _____

Applying Meaning

Read each sentence below. Write "correct" on the answer line if the vocabulary word has been used correctly. Write "incorrect" on the answer line if the vocabulary word has been used incorrectly.

1. The crowd was caught up in the spirit of the Olympic victory and *spontaneously* began to sing the national anthem.

2. The *concatenation* of several poorly tuned instruments confused the choir and effectively ruined the song.

3. A bad cold and high fever have left the captain *predisposed,* but he may be able to receive visitors next week.

4. After ten days of forest fires, the rainstorm seemed *providential.*

5. The graduation speakers were not the top students, so everyone wondered if the choices were *arbitrary.*

6. Because of the *vagaries* of New England weather, you cannot depend on having a warm, sunny vacation even in July.

7. Over the years, his love of sweets and his dislike of exercise made him so *fortuitous* he could hardly get into his clothes.

8. The crash of the airplane resulted in numerous *fatalisms.*

1. _____
2. _____
3. _____
4. _____
5. _____
6. _____
7. _____
8. _____

For each word used incorrectly, write a sentence using the word properly.

_____
_____
_____
_____
_____
_____
_____
_____
_____
_____
_____
_____
_____
_____

Decide which word in parentheses best completes the sentence. Then write the sentence, adding the missing word.

9. Getting the usher to admit us without tickets required us to come up with a _____, like telling him we were part of the entertainment. (concatenation; contrivance)

_____

_____

_____

10. It was pure _____ that brought the two brothers together after twenty years of separation. (serendipity; spontaneity)

_____

_____

_____

11. A _____ burst of laughter from the audience interrupted the actor's speech. (fortuitous; spontaneous)

_____

_____

_____

12. It was a _____ act that held us up in traffic and kept us from boarding the plane that later crashed in thick fog. (predisposed; providential)

_____

_____

_____

Bonus Word

kismet

Another word for fate or fortune is *kismet*. This word took an unusual route into the English language. It may have originated with the Arabic word *qismah,* meaning one's portion or allotment in a distribution. The spelling was altered as it passed through the Persian and Turkish languages into English.

Write a Narrative: Describe something that happened to you that seemed like *kismet.* Use some of the words you studied in this lesson.

Lesson

36

Part A

Name _____

The Greek word *pais*, meaning "child," is the source of the familiar English root *-ped-*. Another common root is *-phil-*, from the Greek word *philos*, meaning "beloved" or "loving." The Latin word *valere*, meaning "to be strong," gives us the root *-val-*. Each vocabulary word in this lesson has one of these roots.

Root	Meaning	English Word
-ped-	child	pedriatics
-phil-	love	bibliophile
-val-	strong	equivalent

Unlocking Meaning

Read the sentences or short passages below. Write the letter for the correct definition of the italicized vocabulary word.

Sometimes Mosi felt that his soccer coach was too demanding and rigid. But at other times, he remembered that the coach always produced winning teams. His *ambivalence* toward the coach was understandable.

 1. (A) conflicting or opposite feelings
    (B) strong sense of duty
    (C) strong dislike
    (D) total devotion

Corrinna is a real *Anglophile*. She spends every summer in England and keeps a scrapbook on the English royal family.

 2. (A) anyone who speaks English
    (B) foreign royalty
    (C) one who travels excessively
    (D) admirer of England's people and English culture

Jon had ignored his studies for most of the term. His efforts to get caught up during the last week of classes were of no *avail*. He failed the course.

 3. (A) remorse or regret
    (B) interest
    (C) use or benefit
    (D) amusement

Ricardo is quite a *bibliophile*. He has spent entire weekends going to yard sales, looking for bargain titles he can add to his library.

 4. (A) storyteller
    (B) lover of books
    (C) student of retail businesses
    (D) someone with strong emotions

Words

ambivalence

Anglophile

avail

bibliophile

countervail

equivalent

pedagogy

pedantic

pediatrics

philanderer

1. _____

2. _____

3. _____

4. _____

To *countervail* her husband's harsh criticism of the service, Ms. Palaski left the overworked waiter a large tip.

5. (A) strengthen
   (B) emphasize
   (C) compensate for
   (D) make clearly apparent

5. _____

I thought the prices in England were a bargain until I learned that it took more than $1\frac{1}{2}$ U.S. dollars to form the *equivalent* of one British pound.

6. (A) equal amount
   (B) form of measurement
   (C) cheap goods
   (D) argument

6. _____

The teacher refused to purchase the textbook because it used a phonics approach to the teaching of reading. She felt this *pedagogy* was not appropriate for her class and instead selected a book that emphasized the use of high-interest literature.

7. (A) expensive item
   (B) childish behavior
   (C) popular opinion
   (D) method of teaching

7. _____

If you ask Lou how to use the computer, be prepared for one of his *pedantic* lectures. When Jerry asked how to keep the screen clean, Lou spent thirty minutes talking about the various sizes and types of screens available.

8. (A) showing off one's learning
   (B) well-prepared
   (C) entertaining and informative
   (D) musical

8. _____

When the hospital's mailroom received packages of stuffed animals and balloons, the clerk assumed they were for someone on the *pediatrics* unit.

9. (A) a group devoted to building maintenance
   (B) branch of medicine devoted to the care of children
   (C) security
   (D) specialists in emergency care

9. _____

Don Juan, the legendary Spanish playboy, is probably the most famous *philanderer* of all times. His romancing of women who found him irresistible is the source of innumerable stories.

10. (A) one who has difficulty expressing himself
    (B) a person who is publicly ridiculed
    (C) someone who has many casual love affairs
    (D) guardian of ancient customs

10. _____

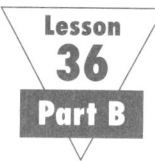
Applying Meaning

Decide which word in parentheses best completes the sentence. Then write the sentence, adding the missing word.

1. When you visit the library, be sure to _____ yourself of the several excellent on-line resources. (avail; countervail)

   _____

   _____

   _____

2. The best gift for a _____ like Janey is a book. (Anglophile; bibliophile)

   _____

   _____

   _____

3. The school counselor said my summerin Mexico was the _____ of a course in Spanish. (ambivalence; equivalent)

   _____

   _____

   _____

4. I was annoyed by her _____ response to Enrique's rather simple question. (pedantic; equivalent)

   _____

   _____

   _____

5. In spite of his _____, Aaron decided to vote in favor of increasing the activity fees. (ambivalence; pedagogy)

   _____

   _____

   _____

Each question below contains a vocabulary word from this lesson. Answer each question "yes" or "no" in the space provided.

6. Would a *philanderer* make a good husband?   6. _____

7. Would you expect to learn a lot from a teacher skilled in *pedagogy*?   7. _____

8. Is an *Anglophile* always skillful in geometry?   8. _____

9. Might a basketball team try to use speed to *countervail* the height advantage of the opponent?

9. _____

10. Would a *pediatric* nurse need to know about childhood diseases?

10. _____

For each question you answered "no," write a sentence using the vocabulary word correctly.

_____

_____

_____

_____

_____

_____

_____

Test-Taking Strategies

Tests are often used to evaluate a student's mastery of standard English grammar and usage. These tests ask you to look at four underlined parts of a sentence and decide if one of the parts contains an error. You are then asked to write the letter for the part containing an error. If there is no error, you write *E*.

Always read the entire sentence before deciding on your answer. To test whether you have identified an error, ask yourself how you would correct the error.

Sample

> **S.** <u>Each camper</u> <u>prepared</u> <u>their</u> own <u>lunch</u>. <u>No Error</u>
>   A   B   C   D   E
>
> S. _____ **C**

Practice: Write the letter for the underlined part of the sentence with an error. If there is no error, write *E*.

1. After the game, <u>each</u> player <u>gave</u> <u>her</u> autograph to Jose and <u>I</u>. <u>No Error</u>
                    A   B   C   D   E

1. _____

2. The <u>children</u> at the new nursery school <u>seems</u> <u>happier</u> than <u>anyone</u>
           A   B   C   D
had hoped at the beginning of the school year. <u>No Error</u>
                                                E

2. _____

3. <u>Appearing suddenly over the horizon</u>, a <u>herd</u> <u>of wild horses</u> <u>galloped</u>
       A   B   C   D
toward the camp. <u>No Error</u>
                  E

3. _____

Name _____

How well do you remember the words you studied in Lessons 34 through 36? Take the following test covering the words from the last three lessons.

Part 1 *Choose the Correct Meaning*

Each question below includes a word in capital letters, followed by four words or phrases. Choose the word or phrase that is <u>closest</u> in meaning to the word in capital letters. Write the letter for your answer on the line provided.

Sample

| **S.** FINISH | (A) enjoy | (B) complete | S. ___**B**___ |
| | (C) destroy | (D) send | |

1. RIVULET   (A) type of fastener   (B) exposure   1. _____
       (C) brook   (D) reverse

2. VAGARY   (A) hidden from view   (B) unpredictable act   2. _____
       (C) cloud formation   (D) misfortune

3. EQUIVALENT   (A) equal in size or   (B) attraction   3. _____
         amount
        (C) expensive   (D) type of money

4. ASCERTAIN   (A) determine   (B) define   4. _____
        (C) send forth   (D) break apart

5. CONFIGURATION   (A) calculation   (B) curved instrument   5. _____
          (C) unfamiliar
           appearance   (D) arrangement

6. RAREFIED   (A) undercooked   (B) genuine   6. _____
        (C) unusual   (D) lofty

7. CONTRIVANCE   (A) means of   (B) plot   7. _____
         transportation
        (C) opposition   (D) failed attempt

8. FORTUITOUS   (A) heavily defended   (B) misfortune   8. _____
        (C) fortunate   (D) influence

9. PEDAGOGY   (A) pleasing melody   (B) sorrowful feelings   9. _____
        (C) method of teaching   (D) study of the feet

Copyright © Glencoe/McGraw-Hill, a division of The McGraw-Hill Companies, Inc.

Go on to next page.

10. BIBLIOPHILE   (A) lover of books   (B) place for keeping records   10. _____

                                 (C) children's doctor   (D) special type of library

11. AVAIL   (A) rolling landscape   (B) ancestor   11. _____
               (C) benefit   (D) carpenter's tool

12. ADHERE   (A) return   (B) decide   12. _____
               (C) admire   (D) cling

13. CEREBRAL   (A) encircled   (B) intellectual   13. _____
               (C) sensational   (D) scientific

14. BROACH   (A) steal   (B) believe   14. _____
               (C) decorate   (D) bring up

15. AMBIVALENCE   (A) conflicting feelings   (B) ambition   15. _____
                             (C) animal-like behavior   (D) friendly feelings

Part 2 Matching Words and Meanings

Match the definition in Column B with the word in Column A.
Write the letter of the correct answer on the line provided.

Column A	Column B	
16. pedantic	a. unrehearsed	16. _____
17. erode	b. series	17. _____
18. recesses	c. parading knowledge	18. _____
19. arbitrary	d. favorable	19. _____
20. spontaneous	e. hidden places	20. _____
21. countervail	f. lover of England	21. _____
22. concatenation	g. wear away	22. _____
23. predisposed	h. make up for	23. _____
24. Anglophile	i. inclined	24. _____
25. providential	j. not determined by rules or reasons	25. _____

Dictionary

Pronunciation Guide

Symbol	Example		Symbol	Example
ă	pat		oi	boy
ā	pay		ou	out
âr	care		ŏŏ	took
ä	father		ōō	boot
ĕ	pet		ŭ	cut
ē	be		ûr	urge
ĭ	pit		th	thin
ī	pie		*th*	this
îr	pier		hw	which
ŏ	pot		zh	vision
ō	toe		ə	about, item
ô	paw			

Stress Marks: ′(primary); ′(secondary), as in **dictionary** (dĭk′shə-nĕr′ē)

A

ab·duct (ăb-dŭkt′) *v.* To carry off (a person) by force; kidnap. **-ab·duct′tion,** *n.*

ab·sti·nence (ăb′stə-nəns) *n.* The act or practice of voluntarily doing without certain foods, drinks, or pleasures.

a·byss (ə-bĭs′) *n.* **1.** An immeasurably deep or seemingly bottomless gulf or pit. **2.** Anything too deep for measurement.

ac·cede (ăk-sēd′) *v.* To give one's consent; agree.

ac·ces·sion (ăk-sĕsh′ən) *n.* **1.** An increase by an addition. **2.** Something that is added or acquired.

ac·tu·ate (ăk′chōō-āt′) *v.* -at·ed, -at·ing. To put into action. **-ac′tu·a′tion,** *n.*

a·cu·i·ty (ə-kyōō′ĭ-tē) *n.* Sharpness or acuteness of vision, thought, or perception; keenness.

ad·a·mant (ăd′ə-mənt, -mănt′) *adj.* Stubbornly unyielding; inflexible. **-ad′a·mant·ly,** *adv.*

ad·duce (ə-dōōs′, ə-dyōōs′) *v.* **-duced, -duc·ing.** To give as a reason, proof, or example. **-ad·duc′i·ble,** *adj.*

a·dept (ə-dĕpt′) *adj.* Highly skilled; expert. **-a·dept′ly,** *adv.* **-a·dept′ness,** *n.*

ad·here (ăd-hîr′) *v.* **-hered, -her·ing. 1.** To stick; cling. **2.** To be a devoted follower; follow closely.

aes·thete (ĕs′thēt) *n.* A person who is or pretends to be highly sensitive to the beauty in art and nature.

af·flu·ent (ăf′lōō-ənt, ə-flōō′-) *adj.* **1.** Wealthy; rich. **2.** Plentiful; abundant. **-af′lu·ent·ly,** *adv.*

al·che·my (ăl′kə-mē) *n.* A medieval chemistry made up of a combination of myths, magic, and science. **-al′che·mist,** *n.*

al·lay (ə-lā′) **1.** To reduce the intensity of; relieve. **2.** To calm or pacify. **-al·lay′er,** *n.*

al·le·vi·ate (ə-lē′vē-āt′) *v.* **-at·ed, -at·ing.** To make more bearable; relieve; lessen. **-al·le′vi·a′tion,** *n.* **-al·le′vi·a′tor,** *n.*

a·loof (ə-loof′) *adj.* Physically or emotionally distant. *-adv.* At a distance.

al·tru·ism (ăl′troo-ĭz′əm) *n.* An unselfish concern for the welfare of others. **-al′tru·is′tic,** *adj.* **-al′tru·is′ti·cal·ly,** *adv.*

a·mass (ə-măs′) *v.* **a·massed, a·mass·ing, a·mass·es.** To collect; accumulate.

am·biv·a·lence (ăm-bĭv′ə-ləns) *n.* The coexistence of conflicting feelings, such as love and hate, toward a person or thing.

a·mor·al (ā-môr′əl, ā-mŏr′-) *adj.* Neither moral nor immoral. Lacking moral awareness.

a·nal·o·gy (ə-năl′ə-jē) *n., pl.* **-gies.** A comparison between two objects that are otherwise quite dissimilar.

an·ar·chy (ăn′ər-kē) *n., pl.* **-chies. 1.** The total absence of government and law. **2.** Political disorder and violence. **3.** Chaos.

an·a·tom·i·cal·ly (ăn′ə-tŏm′ĭ-kəl-lē) *adv.* With reference to the bodily structure of a plant or an animal or its parts. **-an′a·tom′i·cal,** *adj.* **-an′a·tom′ic,** *adj.*

a·ne·mi·a (ə-nē′mē-ə) *n.* A condition in which there is a reduction in red blood cells, resulting in paleness, weakness, and fatigue. **-a·ne′mic,** *adj.*

an·es·thet·ic (ăn′ĭs-thĕt′ĭk) *n.* A substance that causes loss of sensation, with or without loss of consciousness.

An·glo·phile (ăng′glə-fīl) *n.* A person who admires England, its people, culture, customs, etc.

an·i·ma·tion (ăn′ə-mā′shən) *n.* **1.** Liveliness; spirit; vivacity. **2.** The process and technique of preparing animated cartoons.

an·nex (ə-nĕks′, ăn′eks′) *v.* **1.** To incorporate the territory of one state, city, etc., into another. **2.** To add or attach, especially to a larger thing.

an·thro·poid (ăn′thrə-poid′) *adj.* Resembling a human being. *-n.* Any of the most highly developed apes, such as gorillas and chimpanzees.

an·thro·po·mor·phism (ăn′thrə-pə-môr′fĭz′əm) *n.* The attributing of human characteristics to inanimate objects, gods, animals, etc.

an·tic·i·pa·to·ry (ăn-tĭs′ə-pə-tôr′e, -tōr′ē) *adj.* Characterized by advance thought or action.

ap·a·thet·ic (ăp′ə-thĕt′ĭk) *adj.* Feeling or showing no emotion, interest, or concern; indifferent. **ap′a·thet′i·cal·ly,** *adv.*

aph·o·rism (ăf′ə-rĭz′əm) *n.* A short, concise statement of a general truth or opinion.

a·po·lit·i·cal (ā′pə-lĭt′ĭ-kəl) *adj.* **1.** Not interested or involved in politics. **2.** Not having any political importance.

a·poth·e·o·sis (ə-pŏth′ē-ō′sĭs, ăp′ə-thē′ə-sĭs) *n., pl.* **-ses** (sēz′). **1.** Raising a person to the rank of a god. **2.** A perfect example; glorified ideal.

ap·par·ent (ə-păr′ənt, ə-pâr′-) *adj.* **1.** Easily understood; evident; obvious. **2.** Readily seen; visible. **-ap·par′ent·ly,** *adv.* **-ap·par′ent·ness,** *n.*

ap·pe·la·tion (ăp′ə-lā′shən) *n.* A descriptive name, title, or designation.

ap·por·tion (ə-pôr′shən, ə-pōr′-) *v.* To divide and distribute according to a plan; allot.

apt (ăpt) *adj.* **1.** Appropriate; suitable; fitting. **2.** Having a tendency; likely. Quick to learn. **-apt′ly,** *adv.*

ar·bi·trar·y (är′bĭ-trĕr′e) *adj.* **1.** Based on personal opinion or preference rather than on rule or reason. **2.** Based on whim or chance. **-ar′bi·trar′i·ly,** *adv.*

ar·id (ăr′ĭd) *adj.* Having little rainfall; dry and barren; parched.

as·cen·dan·cy (ə-sen′dən-sē) *n.* A position of superiority; dominance. **-as·cen′dant,** *adj.*

as·cer·tain (ăs′ər-tān′) *v.* To find out with certainty; determine. **-as′cer·tain′a·ble,** *adj.* **-as′cer·tain′ment,** *n.*

as·set (ăs′ĕt′) *n.* **1.** Anything owned that is valuable. **2.** A desirable or useful quality or thing; advantage.

as·sid·u·ous (ə-sĭj′ōō-əs) *adj.* Busy; hardworking. **-as·sid′u·ous·ly,** *adv.* **-as·sid′u·ous·ness,** *n.*

as·suage (ə-swāj′) *v.* **-suaged, -suag·ing. 1.** To make less severe; relieve; ease. **2.** To calm. **3.** To satisfy or quench.

as·trin·gent (ə-strĭn′jənt) *adj.* **1.** Sharp; harsh; severe; biting. **2.** Drawing together or con-tracting body tissue.

a·the·ism (ā′thē-ĭz′əm) *n.* The belief that there is no God or gods. **-a′the·ist,** *n.*

a·troc·i·ty (ə-trŏs′ĭ-tē) *n., pl.* **-ties. 1.** Cruel, brutal, or wicked condition, behavior, or quality. **2.** A cruel, brutal, or wicked action or situation.

at·ro·phy (ăt′rə-fē) *v.* **-phied, -phy·ing, -phies.** To waste away, deteriorate. *-n.* A wasting away; deterioration.

a·typ·i·cal (ā-tĭp′ĭ-kəl) *adj.* Unusual; abnormal; irregular. **-a′typ·i·cal′i·ty,** *n.* **-a·typ′i·cal·ly,** *adv.*

au·da·cious (ô-dā′shəs) *adj.* **1.** Bold; daring, **2.** Too daring; insolent. Spirited and original. **au·da′cious·ly,** *adv.* **-au·da′cious·ness,** *n.*

aug·ment (ôg-mĕnt′) *v.* To make larger; increase; enlarge.

aus·pi·ces (ô′spĭ-sĭz, -sēz′) *n.* Support, guidance, or protection.

aus·pi·cious (ô-spĭsh′əs) *adj.* **1.** Favourable. **2.** Marked by success. **-aus·pi′cious·ly,** *adv.* **aus·pi′cious·ness,** *n.*

au·to·crat (ô′tə-krăt′) *n.* A ruler or any person with unlimited power or authority. **-au′to·crat′ic,** *adj.* **-au′to·crat′i·cal·ly,** *adv.*

a·vail (ə-vāl′) *v.* To be of use, help, or advantage to. *-n.* Use or benefit; help; advantage.

B

bale·ful (bāl′fəl) *adj.* Threatening evil; sinister; ominous. **-bale′ful·ly,** *adv.* **-bale′ful·ness,** *n.*

be·set (bĭ-sĕt′) *v.* **-set, -set·ting. 1.** To attack from all sides. **2.** To trouble constantly; harass.

bib·li·o·phile (bĭb′lē-ə-fīl′) *n.* A person who loves or collects books. **-bib′li·oph′i·lism,** *n.*

bland (bland) *adj.* **1.** Not irritating; soothing; mild. **2.** Pleasantly agreeable. **3.** Dull. **-bland′ly,** *adv.* **-bland′ness,** *n.*

bla·zon (blā′zən) *v.* **1.** To display. **2.** To proclaim. **3.** To adorn; embellish. *-n.* **1.** A showy display. **2.** A coat of arms.

boor·ish (boor′ĭsh) *adj.* Rude or bad-mannered. **-boor′ish·ly,** *adv.* **-boor′ish·ness,** *n.*

bowd·ler·ize (bōd′lə-rīz′, boud′-) *v.* **-ized, -iz·ing.** To edit or modify by taking out obscene or objectionable passages.

broach (brōch) *v.* To bring up for the first time for consideration or discussion.

brook (broŏk) *v.* To put up with; tolerate.

brusque (brŭsk) *adj.* Abrupt or rude in manner or speech; blunt. **-brusque′ly,** *adv.* **-brusque′ness,** *n.*

C

can·on (kăn′ən) *n.* **1.** A law or body of laws of a church. **2.** A nonreligious law or code of laws. **3.** A fundamental principle.

ca·pa·cious (kə-pā′shəs) *adj.* Able to contain a great quantity; roomy or spacious. **-ca·pa′cious·ly,** *adv.* **-ca·pa′cious·ness,** *n.*

cap·tious (kăp′shəs) *adj.* Quick to find fault; critical. **-cap′tious·ly,** *adv.* **-cap′tious·ness,** *n.*

cap·ti·vat·ing (kăp′tə-vāt′ĭng) *adj.* Present participle of **captivate.** Attracting and holding by charm, beauty, or excellence **-cap′ti·va′tion,** *n.*

cer·e·bral (sĕr′ə-brəl, sə-rē′-) *adj.* Appealing to the intellect rather than the emotions; intellectual. **-cer·e′bral·ly,** *adv.*

chau·vin·ism (shō′və-nĭz′əm) *n.* Prejudiced belief in the superiority of one's own group, sex, or race. Fanatical patriotism. **-chau′vin·ist,** *n.*

chi·mer·i·cal (kī-mĕr′-i-kəl, -mîr′-, kĭ-) *adj.* **1.** Fantastically improbable. Having a tendency for unrealistic fantasies. **-chi·mer′i·cal·ly,** *adv.*

cir·cum·stan·tial (sûr′kəm-stăn′shəl) *adj.* **1.** Of, relating to, or affected by conditions, factors, or events. **2.** Incidental.

clan·des·tine (klăn-dĕs′tĭn) *adj.* Kept or done in secret, often to hide an improper purpose. **-clan·des′tine·ly,** *adv.* **-clan·des′tine·ness,** *n.*

cog·nate (kŏg′nāt) *-adj.* Related by having the same origin, as certain words. *-n.* A word related to one in another language.

col·lab·o·ra·tion (kə-lăb′ə-rā′shən) *n.* **1.** Working together, especially in an intellectual effort. **2.** Cooperation with the enemy. **-col·lab′o·rate′,** *v.*

col·lu·sion (kə-loo′zhən) *n.* A secret agreement or cooperation between two or more people for an illegal or deceitful purpose; conspiracy.

com·bus·tion (kəm-bŭs′chən) *n.* The process of burning. **-com·bus′ti·ble, -com·bus′tive,** *adj.*

com·mo·di·ous (kə-mō′dē-əs) *adj.* Spacious; roomy. **-com·mo′di·ous·ly,** *adv.* **-com·mo′di·ous·ness,** *n.*

com·ple·men·tar·y (kŏm′plə-mən′tə-rē, trē) *adj.* **1.** Completing. **2.** Supplying mutual needs. **-com′ple·men′ta·ri·ly,** *adv.*

con·cat·e·na·tion (kŏn-kăt′n-ā′shən) *n.* A linked or connected series of things or events.

con·ces·sion (kən-**sĕsh**ʹən) *n.* **1.** A giving in; yielding. **2.** An acknowledgment or admission.

con·di·ment (**kŏn**ʹdə-mənt) *n.* Something used to season food, such as a sauce, relish, or spice.

con·fig·u·ra·tion (kən-fĭgʹyə-**rā**ʹshən) *n.* The arrangement of parts; form or shape determined by the arrangement of parts.

con·i·fer (**kŏn**ʹə-fər, **kō**ʹnə-) *n.* A cone-bearing tree or shrub, chiefly evergreen. **-co·nif**ʹ**er·ous,** *adj.*

con·nois·seur (kŏnʹə-**sûr**ʹ, -**sûr**ʹ) *n.* A person who is an informed judge of something, such as the arts, because of expert knowledge and good taste.

con·stit·u·en·cy (kən-**stĭch**ʹo͞o-ən-sē) *n.* The voters in a district represented by an elected official.

con·strain (kən-**strān**ʹ) *v.* **1.** To force; compel. **2.** To hold back.

con·strict (kən-**strĭkt**ʹ) *v.* To make smaller or narrower by squeezing or binding; contract.

con·tem·pla·tive (kən-**tăm**ʹplə-tĭv, **kŏn**ʹtăm-plā ʹ-) *adj.* Characterized by thoughtful observation and meditation.

con·tend (kən-**tĕnd**ʹ) *v.* **-tend·ed, -tend·ing. 1.** To struggle or fight against difficulties. **2.** To compete. **3.** To argue or dispute.

con·tri·vance (kən-**trī**ʹvəns) *n.* A clever plan, scheme, or device.

co·nun·drum (kə-**nŭn**ʹdrəm) *n.* **1.** A riddle whose answer is a pun or play on words. **2.** Any puzzling problem.

con·vo·lut·ed (**kŏn**ʹvə-lo͞o ʹtĭd) *adj.* **1.** Complicated; intricate. **2.** Twisted; coiled.

cor·po·re·al (kôr-**pôr**ʹē-əl, -**pōr**ʹ-) *adj.* Characteristic of the body; bodily. Of a material nature; tangible.

cor·pu·lence (**kôr**ʹpyə-ləns) **n.** Excessive fatness; obesity. **-cor**ʹ**pu·lent,** *adj.*

cor·pus (**kôr**ʹpəs) *n., pl.* **-po·ra** (-pər-ə). A large or complete collection of writings of a specific type or on a specific subject.

cor·pus·cle (**kôr**ʹpə-səl, -**pŭs**ʹəl) *n.* An unattached cell in the blood or lymph, such as a red or a white blood cell.

coun·ter·vail (kounʹtər-**vāl**ʹ, **koun**ʹtər- vālʹ) *v.* **1.** To make up for; compensate; offset. **2.** To act against with equal power or force; counteract.

cryp·tic (**krĭp**ʹtĭk) *adj.* Having a secret or puzzling meaning; mysterious; baffling. **-cryp**ʹ**ti·cal·ly,** *adv.*

cur·tail (kər-**tāl**ʹ) *v.* To cut short; reduce; shorten. **-cur·tail**ʹ**ment,** *n.*

D

dearth (dûrth) *n.* Scarcity; lack.

de·duce (dĭ-**do͞os**ʹ, -**dyo͞os**ʹ) *v.* **-duced, -duc·ing.** To reach a conclusion from something known; infer. **-de·duc**ʹ**i·ble,** *adj.*

de·file (dĭ-**fīl**ʹ) *v.* **-filed, -fil·ing. 1.** To make filthy or dirty; pollute. **2.** To spoil the pureness of; corrupt.

de·fray (dĭ-**frā**ʹ) *v.* To pay for (the costs or expenses).

deft (dĕft) *adj.* Skillful and quick; masterful. **-deft′ly,** *adv.* **-deft′ness,** *n.*

del·uge (dĕl′yōōj) *n.* **1.** A great flood. **2.** A heavy rainfall; downpour. *-v.* **-uged, -ug·ing. 1.** To flood. **2.** To overwhelm.

de·lu·sive (dĭ-lōō′sɪv) *adj.* **1.** Misleading; deceptive. **2.** False. **-de·lu′sive·ly,** *adv.* **-de·lu′sive·ness,** *n.*

den·i·zen (dĕn′ĭ-zən) *n.* **1.** Inhabitant; occupant. **2.** One who frequents a place.

de·nude (dĭ-nōōd′, -nyōōd′) *v.* **-nud·ed, -nud·ing.** To strip bare.

des·e·crate (dĕs′ĭ-krāt′) *v.* **-crat·ed, -crat·ing.** To treat with disrespect; to violate the sacredness of; defile; profane. **-des′e·cra′tion,** *n.*

des·ti·tute (dĕs′tĭ-tōōt′ -tyōōt′) *adj.* **1.** Lacking the necessities of life; very poor. **2.** Entirely lacking.

de·vi·ous (dē′vē-əs) *adj.* **1.** Untrustworthy; attempting to deceive. Roundabout; wandering. **-de′vi·ous·ly,** *adv.*

di·chot·o·my (dī-kŏt′ə-mē) *n., pl.* **-mies.** Division into two parts or opinions that are usually contradictory.

dire (dīr) *adj.* **-dir·er, dir·est. 1.** Dreadful, horrible. **2.** Urgent; desperate. **-dire′ly,** *adv.* **-dire′ness,** *n.*

dis·cern·i·ble (dĭ-sûr′nə-bəl, -zûr′-) *adj.* Able to be made out clearly. **-dis·cern′i·bly,** *adv.*

dis·con·so·late (dĭs-kŏn′sə-lĭt) *adj.* **1.** Not able to be comforted; dejected. **2.** Gloomy; cheerless. **dis·con′so·late·ly,** *adv.*

dis·pa·rate (dĭs′pər-ĭt, dĭ-spăr′ĭt) *adj.* Different in kind; dissimilar. **-dis′par·ate·ly,** *adv.*

dis·si·dent (dĭs′i-dənt) *adj.* Disagreeing. *-n.* A person who disagrees.

dis·till (dĭ-stĭl′) *v.* **1.** To extract the essential elements of. **2.** To separate by heating until evaporation and condensation take place.

div·i·dend (dĭv′ĭ-dĕnd′) *n.* The money divided among stockholders of a corporation as their share of the profits.

dog·ger·el (dô′gər-əl, dŏg′ər-) *n.* Poetry with little artistic worth that is often humourous, crude, or trivial.

dog·ma (dôg′mə, dŏg′-) *n., pl.* **-mas** or **-ma·ta** (mə-tə). **1.** Official doctrine of a church. **2.** Any principle or doctrine. **-dog·mat′ic,** *adj.*

dra·co·ni·an (drā-kō′nē-ən, drə-) *adj.* Very harsh; severe.

E

e·duce (ĭ-dōōs′, ĭ-dyōōs′) *v.* **e·duced, e·duc·ing.** To bring or draw out; elicit. **-e·duc′i·ble,** *adj.* **-e·duc′tion,** *n.*

e·lix·ir (ĭ-lĭk′sər) *n.* **1.** A remedy believed to cure all ailments. **2.** Substance believed to maintain life forever.

el·lip·sis (ĭ-lĭp′sĭs) *n., pl.* **-ses** (-sēz) The omission of a word or phrase needed for sentence construction but not needed to understand the meaning.

e·lu·ci·date (ĭ-lōō′sĭ-dāt′) *v.* **-dat·ed, -dat·ing.** To make clear; explain. **-e·lu′ci·da′tion,** *n.*

e·man·ci·pate (ĭ-măn′sə-pāt′) *v.* **-pat·ed, -pat·ing.** To liberate from control; free. **-e·man′ci·pa′tion,** *n.*

em·bel·lish (ĕm-**bĕl′**ish) *v.* **1.** To improve the appearance of by decorating. **2.** To add interesting details (often fictitious) to a story.

em·pir·i·cal (ĕm-**pîr′**ĭ-kəl) *adj.* **1.** Relying or based on observation and experiment. **2.** Relying on practical experience rather than on scientific theory.

en·gag·ing (ĕn-**gā′**jĭng) *adj.* Charming; attractive. **-en·gag′ing·ly,** *adv.*

e·nig·ma (ĭ-**nĭg′**mə) *n.* **1.** A puzzling or hard-to-understand person, matter, or thing. **2.** A riddle.

en·tou·rage (**ŏn′**to͞o-räzh′) *n.* A group of associates or attendants.

e·qua·nim·i·ty (ē′kwə-**nĭm′**ĭ-tē, ĕk′wə-) *n.* The quality of remaining calm and even-tempered; composure.

e·qui·lib·ri·um (ē-kwə-**lĭb′**rē-əm, ĕk′wə) *n.,* *pl.* **-ri·ums** or **-ri·a** (-rē-ə) A state of balance between opposing forces.

eq·ui·ty (**ĕk′**wĭ-tē) *n., pl.* **-ties.** The value of a property after the debts are subtracted.

e·quiv·a·lent (ĭ-**kwĭv′**ə-lənt) *adj.* Equal in amount, value, size, force, meaning, etc. *-n.* Something that is equal to another thing.

e·rode (ĭ-**rōd′**) *v.* **e·rod·ed, e·rod·ing. 1.** To wear away gradually. **2.** To eat into; corrode.

er·u·dite (**ĕr′**yə-dīt′, **ĕr′**ə-) *adj.* Characterized by knowledge gained by study or research; learned; scholarly. **-er′u·dite′ly,** *adv.*

eth·nic (**ĕth′**nĭk) *adj.* Relating to groups of people who share common characteristics such as race, nationality, religion, or language.

ev·a·nes·cent (ĕv′ə-**nĕs′**ənt) *adj.* Vanishing or likely to vanish like a vapor. **-ev′a·nes′cence,** *n.* **-ev′a·nes′cent·ly,** *adv.*

e·van·gel·ize (ĭ-**văn′**jə-līz′) *v.* **-ized, -iz·ing.** To preach the gospel. **-e·van′gel·i·za′tion** (-jə-lĭ-**zā′**shən)

ex·em·pli·fy (ĭg-**zĕm′**plə-fī′) *v.* **-fied, -fy·ing, -fies. 1.** To show by example. **2.** To serve as an example of.

ex·or·bi·tant (ĭg-**zôr′**bĭ-tənt) *adj.* Going beyond what is reasonable, just, proper, usual, or fair; excessive. **-ex·or′bi·tant·ly,** *adv.*

ex·ot·ic (ĭg-**zŏt′**ĭk) *adj.* **1.** Foreign. **2.** Strangely beautiful or fascinating. **-ex·ot′i·cal·ly,** *adv.* **-ex·ot′ic·ness,** *n.*

ex·pli·cate (**ĕk′**splĭ-kāt′) *v.* **-cat·ed, -cat·ing.** To explain clearly and thoroughly. **-ex·pli·ca′tion,** *n.*

ex·ploi·ta·tion (ĕk′sploi-**tā′**shən) *n.* **1.** Putting someone or something to productive use. **2.** Use or development for selfish purposes.

ex·ten·u·a·tion (ĭk-sten′yo͞o-**ā′**shən) *n.* **1.** The act of trying to lessen the seriousness of something, especially by giving partial excuses. **-ex·ten′u·at′ing,** *adj.*

ex·trap·o·late (ĭk-**străp′**ə-lāt′) *v.* **-lat·ed, -lat·ing.** To estimate or infer an unknown by extending or projecting known information.

F

fa·tal·ism (**fāt′**l-ĭz′əm) *n.* **1.** The doctrine that all events are predetermined by fate and cannot be changed. **2.** Belief in this doctrine.

fe·lic·i·tous (fĭ-**lĭs′**ĭ-təs) *adj.* **1.** Suitable; appropriate. **2.** Showing an agreeably appropriate manner or style. **-fe·lic′i·tous·ly,** *adv.* **-fe·lic′i·tous·ness,** *n.*

fer·vent (fûr′vənt) *adj.* Having or showing intense emotion or enthusiasm. **-fer′vent·ly,** *adv.* **-fer′vent·ness,** *n.*

fes·ter (fĕs′tər) *v.* **-tered, -ter·ing. 1.** To become infected and form pus. **2.** To become increasingly irritating.

fi·nesse (fə-nĕs′) *n.* **1.** Skill or refinement in doing something. **2.** Skillful handling of a delicate, difficult, or awkward situation.

flawed (flôd) *adj.* Defective; not valid.

flo·res·cent (flô-rĕs′ənt, flə-) *adj.* Blossoming; flowering. **-flo·res′cence,** *n.*

form·a·tive (fôr′mə-tĭv) *adj.* Relating to development or growth. **-form′a·tive·ly,** *adv.*

for·tu·i·tous (fôr-tōō′ĭ-təs, -tyōō′-) *adj.* Happening by chance; accidental. Fortunate; lucky. **-for·tu′i·tous·ly,** *adv.*

frac·tious (frăk′shəs) *adj.* **1.** Inclined to make trouble. **2.** Irritable, cranky. **-frac′tious·ly,** *adv.* **-frac′tious·ness,** *n.*

frag·men·tar·y (frăg′mən-tĕr′e) *adj.* **1.** Consisting of small disconnected parts. **2.** Incomplete. **frag′men·tar′i·ly,** *adv.* **frag′men·tar′i·ness,** *n.*

fu·tile (fyōot′l, fyōo′tĭl′) *adj.* Incapable of having an effective result; useless.

G

gar·gan·tu·an (gär-găn′chōo-ən) *adj.* Gigantic; enormous; huge.

gas·tro·nom·ic (găs′trə-nŏm′ĭk) *adj.* Relating to the science or art of good eating. **-gas′tro·nom′i·cal·ly,** *adv.*

gran·di·ose (grăn′de-ōs′, grăn′de-ōs′) *adj.* **1.** Having greatness of scope; magnificent; grand. **2.** Trying to seem grand; pompous.

grav·i·tate (grăv′ĭ-tāt′) *v.* **-tat·ed, -tat·ing. 1.** To move by the force of gravity. **2.** To be attracted by a strong force.

gul·li·ble (gŭl′ə-bəl) *adj.* Easily deceived or tricked. **-gul′li·bil′i·ty,** *n.* **-gul′li·bly,** *adv.*

H

heart·en·ing (här′tən-ĭng) *v.* Present participle of **hearten.** Encouraging.

hec·tor (hĕk′tər) *n.* A bully *-v.* To threaten or bully.

hu·man·i·tar·i·an (hyōō-măn′ĭ-târ′e-ən) *n.* A person who is devoted to promoting human welfare. *-adj.* Having concern for helping humanity.

hy·brid (hī′brĭd) *n.* **1.** The offspring of two plants or animals of different species, breeds, varieties, etc. **2.** Anything of mixed origin.

I

i·co·nog·ra·phy (ī′kə-nŏg′rə-fe) *n., pl.* **-phies. 1.** The art of illustrating with pictures, figures, etc. **2.** A set of symbolic forms related to a theme of a work of art.

im·per·cep·ti·ble (ĭm′pər-sĕp′tə-bəl) *adj.* So gradual, slight, or subtle as to be barely seen or noticed. **-im′per·cep′ti·bil′i·ty,** *n.* **-im′per·cep′ti·bly,** *adv.*

im·pet·u·ous (ĭm-pəch′ōo-əs) *adj.* **1.** Acting impulsively with little thought; rash. **2.** Impulsive and passionate. **-im·pet′u·ous·ly,** *adv.*

im·ple·ment (ĭm′plə-mənt) *v.* To put into effect; carry out. **-im′ple·men·ta′tion,** *n.* **im′ple·ment′er,** *n.*

im·pli·cate (ĭm′plĭ-kāt′) *v.* **-cat·ed, -cat·ing.** To involve or connect in an incriminatnig way.

im·pon·der·a·ble (ĭm-pŏn′dər-ə-bəl) *adj.* That cannot be weighed, measured, or evaluated with certainty. **-im·pon′der·a·bly,** *adv.*

im·pu·ni·ty (ĭm-pyōō′nĭ-tē) *n., pl.* **-ties.** Freedom from harm, penalty, punishment, or loss.

in·ca·pac·i·tate (ĭn′kə-păs′ĭ-tāt) *v.* **-tat·ed, -tat·ing.** To take away the strength or ability of; disable.

in·cen·di·ar·y (ĭn-sĕn′dē-ĕr′ē) *adj.* Causing or capable of causing fire. *-n.* One who willfully starts fires.

in·cep·tion (ĭn-sĕp′shən) *n.* The beginning of something.

in·ces·sant (ĭn-sĕs′ənt) *adj.* Continuing without interruption; constant; unceasing. **-in·ces′sant·ly,** *adv.*

in·cip·i·ent (ĭn-sĭp′ē-ənt) *adj.* Just beginning to exist or appear. **-in·cip′i·ence,** *n.* **-in·cip′i·ent·ly,** *adv.*

in·cor·po·rate (ĭn-kôr′pə-rāt) *v.* **-rat·ed, -rat·ing. 1.** To unite or work into something that already exists. **2.** To blend or combine thoroughly.

in·ef·fa·ble (ĭn-ĕf′ə-bəl) *adj.* Too overpowering to be described or expressed in words.

in·fi·del (ĭn′fĭ-dəl, -dĕl′) *n.* **1.** A person who does not believe in a particular religion. **2.** A person who has no religious belief.

in·fin·i·tes·i·mal (ĭn′fĭn-ĭ-tĕs′ə-məl) *adj.* Too small to be measured or calculated. **-in′fin·i·tes′i·mal·ly,** *adv.*

in·frac·tion (ĭn-frak′shən) *n.* A violation of a law or rule.

in·im·i·cal (ĭ-nĭm′ĭ-kəl) *adj.* **1.** Harmful; damaging. **2.** Hostile; unfriendly. **-in·im′i·cal·ly,** *adv.*

in·or·di·nate (ĭn-ôr′dn-ĭt, ôrd′nĭt) *adj.* Exceeding proper limits; excessive; immoderate. **-in·or′di·na·cy,** *n.* **-in·or′di·nate·ly,** *adv.*

in·sid·i·ous (ĭn-sĭd′ē-əs) *adj.* **1.** Working in a harmful and stealthy manner. **2.** Treacherous; deceitful. **-in·sid′i·ous·ly,** *adv.*

in·te·gral (ĭn′tĭ-grəl, ĭn-tĕg′rəl) *adj.* **1.** Necessary for completeness; essential. **2.** Complete; whole. **-in′te·gral·ly,** *adv.*

in·ter (ĭn-tûr′) *v.* **-terred, -ter·ing.** To put (a corpse) in a tomb or grave; bury.

in·ter·ces·sion (ĭn′tər-sĕsh′ən) *n.* A plea that is made on behalf of another.

in·tro·spec·tive (ĭn′trə-spĕk′tĭv) *adj.* Inclined to examine one's own thoughts and feelings.

in·vest (ĭn-vĕst′) *v.* **1.** To put money to use to obtain profit. **2.** To give a quality to. **3.** To devote time or effort for future benefit.

i·ras·ci·ble (ĭ-răs′ə-bəl, ī-răs′-) *adj.* Easily angered; irritable. **-i·ras′ci·bil′i·ty, i·ras′ci·ble·ness,** *n.* **-i·ras′ci·bly,** *adv.*

L

lab·y·rinth (lăb′ə-rĭnth′) *n.* A place containing winding, interconnecting passages; a maze.

lav·ish (lăv′ĭsh) *adj.* **1.** Giving or spending in great or generous amounts; extravagant. **2.** More than enough or necessary. **-lav′ish·ly,** *adv.*

lin·go (lĭng′gō) *n., pl.* **-goes. 1.** Language, especially one that is unfamiliar. **2.** The specialized vocabulary of a particular field or group.

lo·gis·tics (lō-jĭs′tĭks, lə-) *n.* The management of details for an operation or event.

lu·cid (lōō′sĭd) *adj.* **1.** Easily understood; clear. **2.** Showing clear thinking; rational; mentally sound. **-lu·cid′i·ty,** *n.*

lu·cre (lōō′kər) *n.* Money or profits.

lu·mi·nar·y (lōō′mə-nĕr′ē) *n., pl.* **-ies.** A person who has achieved fame in a particular field for high achievement; celebrity.

M

Mach·i·a·vel·li·an (măk′ē-ə-vĕl′ē-ən) *adj.* Characterized by trickery and self-interest as a means of achieving one's goals or keeping power.

mag·nan·i·mous (măg-năn′ə-məs) *adj.* **1.** Courageously noble in mind and heart. **2.** Unselfish; generous in forgiving. **-mag·nan′i·mous·ly,** *adv.*

ma·lef·i·cent (mə-lĕf′ĭ-sənt) *adj.* Harmful; evil; hurtful. **-ma·lef′i·cence,** *n.*

man·i·fest (măn′ə-fĕst′) *adj.* Clearly apparent; obvious. *-v.* To make obvious; show plainly. **-man′i·fest′ly,** *adv.*

mar·ti·net (mär′tn-ĕt′) *n.* A strict disciplinarian.

mem·oir (mĕm′wär′, -wôr′) *n.* **1.** An account of events based on the author´s experiences and observations. **2.** Often **memoirs.** An autobiography.

men·dac·i·ty (mĕn-dăs′ĭ-tē) *n., pl.* **-ties. 1.** The quality of being untruthful; untruthfulness. **2.** Given to deception or falsehood.

mer·cu·ri·al (mĕr-kyŏŏr′ē-əl) *adj.* Having rapid and unpredictable changes in mood. **-mer·cu′ri·al·ly,** *adv.*

mer·i·to·ri·ous (mĕr′ĭ-tôr′ē-əs, -tōr′-) *adj.* Having worth, value, or excellence; deserving praise.

me·tic·u·lous (mĭ-tĭk′yə-ləs) *adj.* Extremely or excessively careful about minute details; precise. **-me·tic′u·lous·ly,** *adv.*

mien (mēn) *n.* A person's appearance, bearing, or manner, especially as it shows character or feeling.

mis·an·thrope (mĭs′ən-thrōp, mĭz′-) *n.* A person who hates or distrusts all people. **-mis′an·throp′ic,** *adj.* **-mis′an·throp′i·cal·ly,** *adv.*

mo·bi·lize (mō′bə-līz) *v.* **-lized, -liz·ing.** To assemble and organize for action, use, or war. **-mo′bi·li·za′tion,** *n.*

mod·i·cum (mŏd′ĭ-kəm) *n., pl.* **-cums** or **ca** (-kə). A small or moderate amount.

mon·o·logue (mŏn′ə-lôg′, -lŏg′) *n.* **1.** A long speech made by one person. **2.** A literary or dramatic composition performed by one speaker.

mon·o·the·ism (mŏn′ə-thē-ĭz′əm) *n.* The doctrine or belief that there is only one God. **-mon′o·the′ist,** *n.* **-mon′o·the·is′tic,** *adj.*

muse (myōōz) *n.* **1.** A source of inspiration. **2.** The spirit that inspires a poet or artist.

N

ne·far·i·ous (nə-fâr′ē-əs) *adj.* Extremely wicked; villainous; evil. **-ne·far′i·ous·ly,** *adv.* **-ne·far′i·ous·ness,** *n.*

ne·ol·o·gism (nē-ŏl′ə-jĭz′ĭm) *n.* A new word, expression, or usage, or a new meaning for an existing word. **-ne·ol′o·gist,** *n.*

nu·mi·nous (nōō′mə-nəs, nyōō′-) *adj.* Supernatural; spiritual.

O

op·u·lence (ŏp′yə-ləns) *n.* **1.** Wealth. **2.** Abundance. **-op′u·lent,** *adj.*

os·ten·si·ble (ŏ-stĕn′sə-bəl) *adj.* Apparent; seeming. **-os·ten′si·bly,** *adv.*

ox·y·mo·ron (ŏk′sē-môr′ŏn, -mōr′-) *n., pl.* **-mo·ra** or **-rons.** A figure of speech that combines contradictory words.

P

pan·the·on (păn′thē-ŏn′, -ən) *n.* **1.** A public building in which the famous people of a country are commemorated. **2.** A temple dedicated to all gods.

par·a·digm (păr′ə-dīm′, -dĭm′) *n.* **1.** A list of all forms of a word, to serve as an example for other words. **2.** An example that serves as a model.

pa·ram·e·ter (pə-răm′ĭ-tər) *n.* Limit or boundary; guideline.

par·a·mount (păr′ə-mount′) *adj.* Ranking above all others in importance, concern, influence, etc.; supreme. **-par′a·mount′ly,** *adv.*

par·i·ty (păr′ĭ-tē) *n., pl.* Equality in amount, value, rank, power, etc.

par·lance (pär′ləns) *n.* A way or manner of speaking.

pas·tor·al (păs′tər-əl) *n.* An artistic work that portrays rural life. *-adj.* Charmingly simple and serene.

pa·tri·arch (pā′trē-ärk′) *n.* **1.** Honored leader or founder. **2.** A respected old man of great dignity.

pau·ci·ty (pô′sĭ-tē) *n.* **1.** A small number. **2.** Scarcity; insufficiency.

ped·a·go·gy (pĕd′ə-gō′jē, -gŏj′ē) *n.* The art, science, method, or profession of teaching.

pe·dan·tic (pə-dăn′tĭk) *adj.* **1.** Overemphasizing trivial or minor details. **2.** Parading one's learning. **3.** Unimaginative. **-pe·dan′ti·cal·ly,** *adv.*

pe·di·at·rics (pē′dē-ăt′rĭks) *n. (used with a singular verb).* The branch of medicine dealing with care and treatment of infants and children. **-pe′di·at′ric,** *adj.*

per·di·tion (pər-dĭsh′ən) *n.* The loss of the soul; eternal damnation.

per·pet·u·al (pər-pĕch′ōō-əl) *adj.* **1.** Lasting for an indefinitely long time. **2.** Continuing without interruption. **-per·pet′u·al·y,** adv.

per·plex (pər-plĕks′) *v.* **-plexed, -plex·ing.** To confuse; puzzle; bewilder. **-per·plex′ing·ly,** *adv.*

per·spi·ca·cious (pûr′spĭ-kā′shəs) *adj.* Having keen mental perception and judgment; clear-sighted. **-per′spi·ca′cious·ly,** *adv.*

per·spi·cu·i·ty (pûr′spĭ-kyōō′ĭ-tē) *n.* The quality of being easy to understand; clearness.

phi·lan·der·er (fĭ-lăn′dər-ər) *n.* A man who has many casual or frivolous love affairs.

phi·lan·thro·py (fĭ-lăn′thrə-pē) *n., pl.* **-pies. 1.** Active effort to improve the human condition. **2.** Love of humanity. **-phi·lan′thro·pist,** *n.*

pith·y (**pĭth′ē**) *adj.* **-i·er, -i·est.** Brief and full of meaning. **-pith′i·ly,** *adv.* **-pith′i·ness,** *n.*

plait (plāt, plăt) *n.* A braid. *-v.* To braid.

plau·si·ble (**plô′zə-bəl**) *adj.* Seemingly true, honest, or trustworthy; credible; believable. **-plau′si·bil′i·ty,** *n.*

pli·ant (**plī′ənt**) *adj.* **1.** Easily bent; pliable. **2.** Adaptable. **3.** Easily influenced. **-pli′ant·ly,** *adv.*

por·tent (**pôr′tĕnt′, pōr′-**) *n.* An indication, warning, or sign of something important or disastrous that is about to happen; omen.

prag·mat·ic (**prăg-măt′ĭk**) *adj.* Concerned with facts or actual events; practical. **-prag·mat′i·cal·ly,** *adv.*

prec·e·dent (**prĕs′ĭ-dənt**) *n.* An action, statement, or occurrence that may serve as an example for similar future instances.

pre·co·cious (**prĭ-kō′shəs**) *adj.* Advanced in mental development or maturity. **-pre·co′cious·ly,** *adv.* **-pre·co′cious·ness,** *n.*

pre·dis·posed (**prē′dĭ-spōzd′**) *v. past tense of* **pre·dis·pose.** Inclined to something beforehand; susceptible to.

pre·mier (**prĭ-mîr′, -myîr′, prē′myîr**) *adj.* **1.** First in importance; foremost. **2.** First in time; earliest.

pre·ten·tious (**prĭ-tĕn′shəs**) *adj.* **1.** Making claims to some distinction or importance. **2.** Making an exaggerated outward show; showy. **-pre·ten′tious·ness,** *n.*

pro·di·gious (**prə-dĭj′əs**) *adj.* **1.** Huge; enormous. **2.** Causing amazement; marvelous; wonderful. **-pro·di′gious·ly,** *adv.*

pro·fu·sion (**prə-fyoo′zhən, prō-**) *n.* **1.** An abundance. **2.** A plentiful outpouring or quantity. **3.** Extravagance. **-pro·fuse′,** *adj.*

prop·a·ga·tion (**prŏp′ə-gā′shən**) *n.* Multiplication or increase; the process of spreading; reproduction.

prop·er·ty (**prŏp′ər-tē**) *n., pl.* **-ties.** A characteristic trait, quality, or attribute of a person or thing.

pros·e·ly·tize (**prŏs′ə-lĭ-tīz′**) *v.* **-tized, -tiz·ing.** To attempt to convert from one faith or doctrine to another.

pro·tag·o·nist (**prō-tăg′ə-nĭst**) *n.* The main character in a novel, drama, or other work of literature.

prov·i·den·tial (**prŏv′ĭ-dĕn′shəl**) *adj.* Lucky; favorable; fortunate. Determined by Providence (God). **-prov′i·den′tial·ly,** *adv.*

Q

qualm (kwäm, kwôm) *n.* Feeling of doubt or uneasiness, especially about the rightness of an action.

quan·da·ry (**kwŏn′də-rē, -drē**) *n., pl.* **-ries.** State of uncertainty; dilemma.

quer·u·lous (**kwĕr′ə-ləs, kwĕr′yə-**) *adj.* Complaining; ill-tempered. **-quer′u·lous·ly,** *adv.* **quer′u·lous·ness,** *n.*

R

rar·e·fied (**râr′ə-fīd′**) *adj.* **1.** Not dense; thin. **2.** Interesting to a small, select group. **3.** Elevated in character or style.

re·cede (**rĭ-sēd′**) *v.* **-ced·ed, -ced·ing. 1.** To move back or away. **2.** To retreat or withdraw.

re·cep·ta·cle (**rĭ-sĕp′tə-kəl**) *n.* A container for holding something.

re·cess·es (re′sĕs′ĭz, rĭ′sĕs′ĭz) *n.* **1.** Remote, inner, or hidden places. **2.** Indentations or small hollows.

re·cu·per·ate (rĭ-kōō′pə-rāt′, -kyōō′-) *v.* To get well again; recover. -re·cu′per·a′tion, *n.*

re·frac·to·ry (rĭ-frăk′tə-rē) *adj.* Difficult to control; stubbornly disobedient.

re·ga·lia (rĭ-gāl′yə, -gā′lē-ə) *pl. n. (used with a sing. or pl. verb)* **1.** The emblems and symbols of royalty or rank. **2.** Splendid clothes; finery.

re·gime (rā-zhēm′, rĭ-) *n.* **1.** The government in power. **2.** A system of government.

reg·i·men (rĕj′ə-mən, -mĕn′) *n.* A regular system of diet, exercise, rest, etc., to improve or promote health.

reg·i·ment (rĕj′ə-mənt) *v.* **1.** To put into a systematic order. **2.** To subject to strict discipline and control. -*n.* A military unit.

reg·nant (rĕg′nənt) *adj.* **1.** Reigning; ruling. **2.** Predominant. **3.** Widespread.

re·lu·cent (rĭ-loo′sənt) *adj.* Reflecting light; bright; shining.

ren·der·ing (rĕn′dər-ĭng) *n.* A representation or interpretation, as in art or music.

rep·li·ca (rĕp′lĭ-kə) *n.* **1.** A copy or reproduction of a work of art. **2.** Any close copy or reproduction; copy.

re·pu·di·ate (rĭ-pyōō′dē-āt) *v.* -at·ed, -at·ing. **1.** To reject the validity of. **2.** To reject as untrue or unjust. **3.** To refuse to have any dealings with.

re·sid·u·al (rĭ-zĭj′oo-əl) *adj.* Left over after part is taken away; remaining. -*n.* What is left over at the end of a process; remainder.

res·ti·tu·tion (rĕs′tĭ-tōō′shən, tyōō′-) *n.* **1.** Reimbursement for loss or damage; compensation. **2.** Restoration to the owner of something that was taken.

ret·i·nue (rĕt′n-ōō′, -yōō′) *n.* A group of attendants accompanying an important person.

ret·ro·spect (rĕt′rə-spĕkt′) *n.* A review or contemplation of the past. -ret′ro·spec′tive, *n., adj.*

rev·el (rĕv′əl) *v.* -eled, -el·ing; also -elled, -el·ling. **1.** To take great pleasure. **2.** To engage in noisy celebration. *n.* Merrymaking.

riv·u·let (rĭv′yə-lĭt) *n.* A small stream or brook.

ru·di·men·ta·ry (rōō′də-mĕn′tə-rē, -mĕn′trē) *adj.* Having or related to the fundamental facts or principles; elementary.

S

sac·ri·lege (săk′rə-lĭj) *n.* Violation or misuse of something sacred.

sar·don·ic (sär-dŏn′ĭk) *adj.* Scornfully or bitterly mocking; sarcastic. -sar·don′i·cal·ly, *adv.*

sa·ti·ate (sā′shē-at′) *v.* -at·ed, -at·ing. **1.** To satisfy fully. **2.** To satisfy to excess.

sat·ur·nine (săt′ər-nīn′) *adj.* Having a gloomy, sullen, or sluggish temperament. -sat′ur·nine′ly, *adv.*

sa·vant (să-vänt′) *n.* A learned person; scholar.

scin·til·late (sĭn′tl-āt′) *v.* -lat·ed, -lat·ing. **1.** To sparkle or shine. **2.** To be animated, brilliant, and witty.

sé·ance (sā′äns′) *n.* A meeting in which people try to communicate with the spirits of the dead.

se·date (sĭ-**dāt′**) *adj.* Quiet; calm; dignified and composed.

sed·a·tive (**sĕd′**ə-tĭv) *n.* A medicine that calms, soothes, and lessens anxiety. *-adj.* Soothing; calming.

sed·en·tar·y (**sĕd′**n-tĕr′ē) *adj.* Requiring or characterized by much sitting.

sed·i·ment (**sĕd′**ə-mənt) *n.* Matter that settles to the bottom of a liquid.

se·duce (sĭ-**do͞os′**, -dyo͞os′) *v.* **-duced, -duc·ing.** **1.** To persuade or tempt into wrongdoing. **2.** To tempt with the hope of reward.

ser·en·dip·i·ty (sĕr′ən-**dĭp′**ĭ-tē) *n.* The power or ability to make fortunate discoveries by accident.

sil·hou·ette (sĭl′o͞o-**ĕt′**) *n.* **1.** The outline of a figure filled in with solid color, usually black. **2.** A profile. *-v.* To show in silhouette.

skep·ti·cism (**skĕp′**tĭ-sĭz′əm) *n.* A questioning or doubting attitude. **-skep′ti·cal,** *adj.*

smug (smŭg) *adj.* **smug·ger, smug·gest.** Showing or feeling offensive self-satisfaction. **-smug′ly,** *adv.* **-smug′ness,** n.

so·lid·i·fy (sə-**lĭd′**ə-fī) *v.* **-fied, -fy·ing, -fies. 1.** To make solid, compact, or hard. **2.** To make or become strong or united.

sol·u·ble (**sŏl′**yə-bəl) *adj.* Capable of being solved. **-sol′u·ble·ness,** *n.* **-sol′u·bly,** *adv.*

sol·vent (**sōl′**vənt, sôl′-) *adj.* Able to pay all one's debts.

som·ber (**sŏm′**bər) *adj.* **1.** Dark and gloomy. **2.** Dismal; sad. **-som′ber·ly,** *adv.* **-som′ber·ness,** *n.*

sparse (spärs) *adj.* **-spars·er, spars·est.** Thinly spread; not dense. **-sparse′ly,** *adv.* **-sparse′ness,** *n.*

spe·cious (**spē′**shəs) *adj.* **1.** Seeming true or correct but actually false. **2.** Deceptively attractive. **-spe′cious·ly,** *adv.* **-spe′cious·ness,** *n.*

spec·u·late (**spĕk′**yə-lāt′) *v.* **-lat·ed, -lat·ing.** To meditate on a subject; to wonder.

spon·ta·ne·ous (spŏn-**tā′**nē-əs) *adj.* **1.** Happening by impulse or desire; not planned. **2.** Happening without any apparent outside cause. **-spon·ta′ne·ous·ly,** *adv.*

spo·rad·ic (spə-**răd′**ĭk, spô-) *adj.* Happening at irregular intervals; not constant or regular; periodic. **-spo·rad′i·cal·ly,** *adv.*

spu·ri·ous (spyo͞or′ē-əs) *adj.* Not genuine; false. **-spu′ri·ous·ly,** *adv.* **-spu′ri·ous·ness,** *n.*

stat·ure (**stăch′**ər) *n.* **1.** The height of a person or animal in a standing position. **2.** An achieved level of esteem or status.

stat·ute (**stăch′**o͞ot) *n.* **1.** A law passed by a legislative body. **2.** An established rule or law regulating an organization.

sten·to·ri·an (stĕn-**tôr′**ē-ən, -tōr′-) *adj.* Extremely loud.

strife (strīf) *n.* **1.** Fight, struggle, or quarrel. **2.** Bitter conflict. **3.** A competition between rivals.

strin·gent (**strĭn′**jənt) *adj.* Strict; severe. **-strin′gent·ly,** *adv.*

styl·ized (**stī′**līzd′) *v.* Past tense of **stylize, -iz·ing, -iz·es.** To design according to a particular style rather than according to nature.

sub·lime (sə-**blīm**′) *adj.* **1.** Noble; majestic. **2.** Inspiring admiration or awe. **3.** Not to be excelled; supreme. **-sub·lime′ly,** *adv.*

sub·sid·ar·y (səb-**sĭd**′ē-ĕr′ē) *adj.* **1.** Of lesser importance. **2.** Acting to help; auxiliary. *-n.* A company owned or controlled by another company.

sump·tu·ous (**sŭmp**′chŏŏ-əs) *adj.* Excessively costly, rich, luxurious, or magnificent. **-sump′tu·ous·ly,** *adv.* **-sump′tu·ous·ness,** *n.*

su·per·sede (sŏŏ′pər-**sēd**′) *v.* **-sed·ed, -sed·ing.** To take the place of; replace.

su·pine (sŏŏ-**pīn**′, **sŏŏ**′pīn′) *adj.* Inactive; passive. **-su·pine′ly,** *adv.* **-su·pine′ness,** *n.*

sup·pli·cate (**sŭp**′lĭ-kāt′) *v.* **-cat·ed, -cat·ing.** **1.** To ask for humbly or earnestly, as by praying. **2.** To beg. **-sup′pli·ca′tion,** *n.*

sur·rep·ti·tious (sûr′əp-**tĭsh**′əs) *adj.* **1.** Done, made, or gotten in a secret, stealthy way. **2.** Acting in a stealthy way. **-sur′rep·ti′tious·ly,** *adv.*

sus·cep·ti·ble (sə-**sĕp**′tə-bəl) *adj.* **1.** Easily affected or influenced. **2.** Impressionable; sensitive. **-sus·cep′ti·ble·ness,** *n.*

syb·a·rite (**sĭb**′ə-rīt) *n.* A person who is fond of pleasure and luxury. **syb′a·rit′ic,** *adj.*

T

tau·tol·o·gy (tô-**tŏl**′ə-jē) *n., pl.* **-gies.** The needless repetition of an idea in different words.

taw·dry (**tô**′drē) *adj.* Cheap and tastelessly showy. **-taw′dri·ly,** *adv.* **-taw′dri·ness,** *n.*

ten·a·ble (**tĕn**′ə-bəl) *adj.* **1.** Capable of being maintained in argument; reasonable. **2.** Capable of being defended against attack. **-ten′a·bly,** *adv.*

te·na·cious (tə-**nā**′shəs) *adj.* **1.** Holding firmly. **2.** Tending to retain well. **3.** Adhesive. **4.** Persistent; stubborn. **-te·na′cious·ly,** *adv.*

ten·ant (**tĕn**′ənt) *n.* A person who pays rent to occupy or use the property owned by another, such as land or a building.

ten·u·ous (**tĕn**′yŏŏ-əs) *adj.* **1.** Lacking substance; flimsy; weak. **2.** Slender or delicate. **-ten′u·ous·ly,** *adv.* **-ten′u·ous·ness,** *n.*

ten·ure (**tĕn**′yər, -yŏŏr′) *n.* **1.** The holding of something, such as property or office. **2.** The length of time something is held.

terse (tûrs) *adj.* Brief and to the point; concise. **-terse′ly,** *adv.* **-terse′ness,** *n.*

the·oc·ra·cy (thē-**ŏk**′rə-sē) *n., pl.* **-cies. 1.** A government ruled or subject to religious authority. **2.** A country ruled in this way.

the·o·log·i·cal (thē′ə-**lŏj**′ĭ-kəl) *adj.* Relating to the study of the nature of God and religious truth.

ther·a·peu·tic (thĕr′ə-**pyŏŏ**′tĭk) *adj.* Serving to heal, cure, or maintain health. **-ther′a·peu′ti·cal·ly,** *adv.*

trans·lu·cent (trăns-**lŏŏ**′sənt, trănz-) *adj.* Allowing light to pass through but not allowing objects on the other side to be clearly seen.

trib·u·la·tion (trĭb′yə-**lā**′shən) *n.* Great misery or suffering; distress.

trun·cate (**trŭng**′kāt) *v.* **-cat·ed, -cat·ing.** To shorten or make smaller by cutting off a part. **-trun′ca′ted,** *adj.*

tu·mult (**tŏŏ**′mŭlt′, **tyŏŏ**′-) *n.* **1.** The din and commotion of a crowd; uproar. **2.** A disorderly disturbance. **3.** Agitation of the mind or feelings.

U

u·nan·i·mous (yōō-**năn**′ə-məs) *adj.* Being in or showing complete agreement.

un·found·ed (ŭn-**found**′dĭd) *adj.* Not based on fact or truth; baseless. **-un·found′ed·ly,** *adv.* **-un·found′ed·ness,** *n.*

V

va·ga·ry (**vā**′gə-rē, və-**gâr**′ē) *n., pl.* **-ries.** An erratic or unpredictable act, idea, or happening; whim.

van·guard (**văn**′gärd) *n.* **1.** The part of the army that goes ahead of the main force. **2.** The leading position in a trend or movement; forefront.

ven·er·ate (**věn**′ə-rāt′) *v.* **-at·ed, -at·ing.** To regard with deep respect and reverence; revere.

ver·nac·u·lar (vər-**năk**′yə-lər) *n.* **1.** The common, everyday language spoken by a people. **2.** The standard native language of a country or place.

vil·i·fi·ca·tion (**vĭl**′ə-fĭ-kā′shən) *n.* The act of making vicious and damaging statements about. **-vil′i·fy, -fied, -fy·ing, -fies,** *v.*

vir·tu·o·so (vûr′chōō-**ō**′sō, -zō) *n., pl.* **-sos** or **-si** (-sē). **1.** A musician with great skill, technique, or style, **2.** A person having great skill in some activity.

vo·ta·ry (**vō**′tĕ-rē) *n., pl.* **-ries. 1.** A faithful follower. **2.** A person who lives a life of religious service.

W

wrought (rôt) *adj.* Formed; made; crafted.

Z

zeal·ous (**zĕl**′əs) *adj.* Filled with intense desire or enthusiasm. **-zeal′ous·ly,** *adv.* **-zeal′ous·ness,** *n.*

Standardized Test Practice

In lessons 1 to 36, you have concentrated on building vocabulary, a skill that is an important aid in reading comprehension. However, the competent reader must master a variety of other skills. These include the following:

• **Identifying main and subordinate ideas**—deciding what the most important idea in the selection is and what items support that idea

Examples:

Main idea	Marcel Marceau is the master of mime, the wordless theater.
Subordinate ideas	Marceau admired Charlie Chaplin, Buster Keaton, and the Marx Brothers, all of whom used mime in their performances.
	Marceau tells most of his stories through Bip the clown, a character he created.
	Marceau's aim is to make his audiences see, feel, and hear the invisible.

• **Deciding on an appropriate title**—choosing a title that is closely related to the main idea of a selection

• **Drawing inferences**—coming to a conclusion that is not directly stated but is based on information given

Example:

If a woman is clasping her purse tightly and looking around her, you can infer that she is afraid her purse will be stolen.

• **Locating details**—scanning a selection to find the answer to a specific question

The following pages will give you a chance to practice the skills you use when you read. The questions they contain are the kinds of questions you will be asked to answer on a standardized test.

The reading selections include passages from science and social studies texts as well as informative essays and short narratives.

Reread the selection "Cuna Creations" on page 1 and answer the following questions. Circle the letter that precedes the BEST answer to each question.

1. What is the main idea of the selection?

   A. The Cuna people inhabit the San Blas islands.

   B. Molas have been an art form among the Cuna for thousands of years.

   C. Molas, colorful hand-stitched cloths, are a source of income for the Cuna people.

   D. Intricately patterned molas, besides being useful, have a deeply religious function in Cuna society.

2. What kinds of designs are most prominent in molas?

   A. Abstract religious symbols

   B. Intricate geometrical patterns

   C. Representations of heavenly bodies

   D. Stylized images of animals and plants

3. Why did Cuna women create molas?

   A. Molas were created as clothing to replace body paint.

   B. Missionaries and traders taught them how to create salable items.

   C. Cuna women wanted to preserve the art form used by their ancestors.

   D. Cuna women needed unique items that would bring necessary income.

4. What does the word *economy* mean, as it is used in the fifth paragraph?

   A. Thrift and frugality

   B. Financial system

   C. Investment goal

   D. Profitability

5. Which of the following statements is true?

   A. An elaborate mola has been created from a single piece of cloth.

   B. Today Cuna women help men with the duties of farming and building.

   C. Molas remain an important part of the traditional dress of Cuna women.

   D. The demand for molas has become so great that a mola factory has been established.

6. If you place the following items in chronological order, which one is first?

   A. The sale of molas becomes an important source of income.

   B. Cuna women paint their bodies with colorful designs.

   C. Missionaries and traders visit the San Blas islands.

   D. Cuna women create molas to use as clothing.

Reread the selection "The Terra-Cotta Army of Shi Huang Di" on page 57 and answer the following questions. Circle the letter that precedes the BEST answer to each question.

1. When was the terra-cotta army of Shi Huang Di discovered?

   A. About 1500 years after the army had been buried

   B. During the occupation after World War II

   C. During the young emperor's reign

   D. In 1974

2. Which of the following statements is true?

   A. Shi Huang Di urged all of his subjects to follow the teachings of Confucius.

   B. Shi Huang Di completed the Great Wall and unified China under one rule.

   C. Shi Huang Di was a benevolent and enlightened ruler.

   D. Shi Huang Di ruled for half a century.

3. Why is the terra-cotta army of Shi Huang Di remarkable?

   A. The warriors' armor, the horses, and the chariots are all richly detailed.

   B. The weapons of the warriors are still functional after 2000 years.

   C. Its 7000 life-size warriors each have distinctive features.

   D. All of the above reasons are true.

4. Which of the following was NOT accomplished during the reign of Shi Huang Di?

   A. The standard of living of peasants was raised.

   B. Weights and measures were standardized.

   C. A network of roads and canals was built.

   D. The system of writing was unified.

5. What is meant by the *vanguard* of an army?

   A. The mounted troops

   B. The main body of troops

   C. The troops guarding the general

   D. The troops that precede the main body

Reread the selection "Zlata's Diary: A Child's Life in Sarajevo" on page 85 and answer the following questions. Circle the letter that comes before the BEST answer to each question.

1. From the details in the second paragraph, what can you infer about Zlata's early life?

   A. Zlata's family was extremely poor.

   B. Zlata enjoyed a comfortable life style.

   C. The Filipovic family was very wealthy.

   D. Zlata's parents were important in political circles

2. What makes Zlata's diary especially touching?

   A. She includes dramatic descriptions of battles.

   B. Her vocabulary is very impressive.

   C. She describes ordinary things.

   D. She uses poetic language.

3. Which of the following statements is NOT true?

   A. Zlata got the inspiration for writing her diary from Anne Frank's *Diary of a Young Girl*.

   B. A French publisher helped Zlata and her family immigrate to France.

   C. Zlata's diary records her growth from childhood to adolescence.

   D. Zlata and Anne Frank met in France.

4. According to Zlata, what group is responsible for the warfare?

   A. The Serbs

   B. Politicians

   C. The Croats

   D. The Muslims

5. As it is used in the selection, what does the word *entries* mean?

   A. Permission to enter

   B. Recording of events

   C. Invasion and occupation

   D. Admittance into a facility

Read the selection "Peaks and Politics" on page 99 and answer the following questions.

1. In what year was Grand Teton National Park, including the gift of Rockefeller, finally created?

   A. 1926

   B. 1929

   C. 1942

   D. 1950

2. Why had Rockefeller's gift of land for a national park been refused?

   A. The country had enough land set aside for parks.

   B. Western settlers and cattle ranch owners wanted the land for their own uses.

   C. The upkeep of the park would be too great a drain on government resources.

   D. Poorer citizens did not want the wealthy Rockefeller to have anything to say about the land.

3. What led to the establishment of dude ranches?

   A. Cattle breeders needed a new source of income when beef prices plunged.

   B. Many Americans were looking for new and different vacation experiences.

   C. Cowboys had found work elsewhere, and the ranch owners needed more workers.

   D. Ranch owners wanted to provide city dwellers with an opportunity to work outdoors.

4. What would be another appropriate title for this selection?

   A. Ranchers and Cowboys

   B. The Great Outdoors

   C. A Disputed Gift

   D. National Parks

5. How does a person show *altruism?*

   A. By always speaking the truth

   B. By trusting the opinions of others

   C. By showing a tolerance for high altitudes

   D. By giving without expecting a gift in return

Read the following passages and answer the questions that follow.

Passage I

It is simple enough to say that books have classes—fiction, biography, poetry—we should separate them and take from each what it is right that each should give us. Yet few people ask from books what books can give us. Most commonly we come to books with blurred and divided minds, asking of fiction that it shall be true, of
5 poetry that it shall be false, of biography that it shall be flattering, of history that it shall enforce our own prejudices. If we could banish all such preconceptions when we read, that would be an admirable beginning. Do not dictate to your author; try to become him. Be his fellow-worker and accomplice. If you hang back, and reserve and criticize at first, you are preventing yourself from getting the fullest possible
10 value from what you read. But if you open your mind as widely as possible, then signs and hints of almost imperceptible fineness, from the twist and turn of the first sentences, will bring you into the presence of a human being unlike any other. Steep yourself in this, acquaint yourself with this, and soon you will find that your author is giving you, or attempting to give you, something far more definite. The thirty-two
15 chapters of a novel—if we consider how to read a novel first—are an attempt to make something as formed and controlled as a building: but words are more impalpable than bricks; reading is a longer and more complicated process than seeing. Perhaps the quickest way to understand the elements of what a novelist is doing is not to read, but to write; to make your own experiment with the dangers and difficul-
20 ties of words. Recall, then, some event that has left a distinct impression on you—how at the corner of the street, perhaps, you passed two people talking. A tree shook; an electric light danced; the tone of the talk was comic, but also tragic; a whole vision, an entire conception, seemed contained in that moment.

But when you attempt to reconstruct it in words, you will find that it breaks into
25 a thousand conflicting impressions. Some must be subdued; others emphasized; in the process you will lose, probably, all grasp upon the emotion itself. Then turn from your blurred and littered pages to the opening pages of some great novelist—Defoe, Jane Austen, Hardy. Now you will be better able to appreciate their mastery. It is not merely that we are in the presence of a different person—Defoe, Jane Austen, or
30 Thomas Hardy—but that we are living in a different world. Here, in *Robinson Crusoe*, we are trudging a plain high road; one thing happens after another; the fact and the order of the fact is enough. But if the open air and adventure mean everything to Defoe they mean nothing to Jane Austen. Hers is the drawing-room, and people talking, and by the many mirrors of their talk revealing their characters. And
35 if, when we have accustomed ourselves to the drawing-room and its reflections, we turn to Hardy, we are once more spun around. The moors are round us and the stars are above our heads. The other side of the mind is now exposed—the dark side that comes uppermost in solitude, not the light side that shows in company. Our relations are not towards people, but towards Nature and destiny. Yet different as these worlds
40 are, each is consistent with itself. The maker of each is careful to observe the laws of his own perspective, and however great a strain they may put upon us they will never

confuse us, as lesser writers so frequently do, by introducing two different kinds of reality into the same book. Thus to go from one great novelist to another—from Jane Austen to Hardy, from Peacock to Trollope, from Scott to Meredith—is to be
45 wrenched and uprooted; to be thrown this way and then that. To read a novel is a difficult and complex art. You must be capable not only of great finesse of perception, but of great boldness of imagination, if you are going to make use of all that the novelist—the great artist—gives you.

–from *The Second Common Reader* by Virginia Woolf

Passage II

Literature was born not the day when a boy crying *wolf, wolf* came running out of the Neanderthal valley with a big gray wolf at his heels: literature was born on the day when a boy came crying *wolf, wolf* and there was no wolf behind him. That the poor little fellow because he lied too often was finally eaten up by a real beast is
5 quite incidental. But here is what is important. Between the wolf in the tall grass and the wolf in the tall story there is a shimmering go-between. That go-between, that prism, is the art of literature.

Literature is invention. Fiction is fiction. To call a story a true story is an insult to both art and truth. Every great writer is a great deceiver, but so is that arch-cheat
10 Nature. Nature always deceives. From the simple deception of propagation to the prodigiously sophisticated illusion of protective colors in butterflies or birds, there is in Nature a marvelous system of spells and wiles. The writer of fiction only follows Nature's lead.

Going back for a moment to our wolf-crying woodland little woolly fellow, we
15 may put it this way: the magic of art was in the shadow of the wolf that he deliberately invented, his dream of the wolf; then the story of his tricks made a good story. When he perished at last, the story told about him acquired a good lesson in the dark around the camp fire. But he was the little magician. He was the inventor.

There are three points of view from which a writer can be considered: he may be
20 considered as a storyteller, as a teacher, and as an enchanter. A major writer combines these three-storyteller, teacher, enchanter—but it is the enchanter in him that predominates and makes him a major writer.

–from *Lectures on Literature* by Vladimir Nabokov

Circle the letter that precedes the BEST answer to each of the following questions.

Questions about Passage I

1. What is the author's attitude toward most people's reading habits?
    A. strong admiration
    C. mild disdain
    B. intense animosity
    D. passive indifference

2. In lines 26 through 39, what does the author describe?
    A. the setting of each author's novels
    B. the style of writing each author uses
    C. the culture in which each author lived
    D. the location in which we read each author's novels

3. What does the author consider the greatest skill of a quality novelist?
    A. the ability to create an imaginary world
    B. the ability to tell the reader an interesting story
    C. the ability to maintain uniformity throughout the book
    D. the ability to teach a lesson and inspire the reader to do good

Questions about Passage II

4. Which kind of writing does the author of this passage esteem most highly?
    A. history texts
    C. fictional stories
    B. magazine interviews
    D. scientific reports

5. In lines 13 through 17, what reference does the author make to illustrate his point?
    A. a well-known author
    C. a historical event
    B. a famous story
    D. an exciting adventure

6. In line 17 of the passage, what skill does the author emphasize by referring to the boy as "the little magician"?
    A. that of a creator
    C. that of a hunter
    B. that of a writer
    D. that of an entertainer

Read the following article and answer the questions that follow.

from English Settlers in Virginia
by Donald A. Ritchie and Albert S. Broussard

The English established their first permanent settlement in the Americas in 1607. However, English merchants and adventurers had been engaged in failed efforts since the late 1500s.

With the permission of Queen Elizabeth, Sir Walter Raleigh raised money to establish a colony, and in 1585 a small group of men sailed for the Americas. They landed on Roanoke Island near the coast of present-day North Carolina. In less than a year, they had run short of food, and when an English ship unexpectedly arrived, all the colonists boarded and returned to England.

Lost Colony at Roanoke

Raleigh tried again in 1587, sending an expedition of ninety-one men, seventeen women, and two children under the leadership of John White. Raleigh hoped this group would form the nucleus of a farming community. Shortly after arriving, one of the women gave birth to Virginia Dare, the first American-born child of English parents. Virginia was White's grandchild.

White left his daughter, granddaughter, and the rest of the colonists, after several weeks, to return to England for supplies and more settlers. He hoped to return in a few months, but hostilities between England and Spain prevented his return.

When he did return in 1590, he found the island completely deserted with no trace of the settlers. No trace of the colonists has been found. The fate of the "Lost Colony" remains a mystery.

Staking a Claim in the Americas

The possibility of riches in America commanded the attention of the English. By 1600 Spain had gained a fortune from the gold and silver in its American colonies in western North America, present-day Florida, South America, and the Caribbean. The English king, James I, could not afford to send ships and supplies to America, and English nobles were unwilling to risk their private wealth. English merchants, however, were eager for a share in the rich new continent. In 1606 merchants in the cities of London and Plymouth came up with a new way to share the costs of starting a colony.

The Virginia Companies

The merchants formed two companies, the Virginia Company of Plymouth and the Virginia Company of London. Each was a joint-stock company that sold shares to investors. Each investor contributed only a small part of the cost. If the company's project succeeded, investors shared the profits. If it failed, they lost only as much money as they had put in.

Upon receiving official permission from King James I, each company received a charter—a document that let them settle and trade in a certain area in the Americas. The London group's charter permitted it to settle land between present-day North Carolina and the Potomac River. The land was named Virginia. The charter granted colonists of Virginia the same rights as English citizens.

The Settlement of Jamestown

In December 1606 the London Company sent three ships—the *Discovery,* the *Susan Constant,* and the *Godspeed*—to start a colony in North America. The 144 men—no women were sent—faced a rough, stormy voyage. More than forty died at sea. Finally, in April 1607, the ships reached Virginia.

They sailed into Chesapeake Bay and up a wide river that the colonists named the James River after their king. They landed on a peninsula sixty miles (96 km) up the river, and established their settlement, named Jamestown.

Jamestown Faces Problems

Jamestown's location was a good spot from which to keep a lookout for Spanish ships. It was also a good spot to trade with nearby Native Americans in. It had serious drawbacks, however. The swampy land was filled with mosquitoes and lacked good drinking water. As a result, many colonists died of malaria or typhoid fever.

Jamestown faced another serious problem. Its colonists knew nothing about living in a wilderness. Many of them were gentlemen from wealthy English families. They had never worked and had no practical skills. They had come to America for gold and adventure, not to cut wood, build homes, or plant crops. By September 1607 about half the colonists had died from the hard life, and by the next January only thirty-eight were still alive.

John Smith Takes Charge

Governing Jamestown was perhaps the biggest problem colonists faced. The London Company had originally set up a board of thirteen to rule the settlers. The board members quarreled, and some quit. Many of the colonists refused to plant crops and only searched for gold. Without a strong leader, Jamestown's future was in danger.

Captain John Smith, a brave adventurer, stepped forward to take charge. Smith had no patience with the colonists' complaints. He promptly ordered the people—including the idle gentlemen—to build houses and fortifications, dig wells, clear fields, and plant crops. He made it clear that "he that will not work shall not eat."

Smith also bargained for supplies with the local Native Americans, members of the Powhatan confederacy. Smith claimed to have been captured by the Powhatans but was later released. He said that Pocahontas—daughter of the chief called Powhatan—had begged for his life. Later Pocahontas married colonist John Rolfe.

The "Starving Time"

Corn and fresh water from the Native Americans helped the colony survive. Under John Smith's leadership, conditions in Jamestown improved. About 500 new settlers—this time including women—came from England to join the colony in 1609. Unfortunately, Smith was hurt in a gunpowder explosion and had to return to England for medical treatment.

Once again, the colony faced hardship. That winter the food supply ran low, and people fought one another for roots, acorns, and even insects. Only sixty settlers survived the "starving time," the winter of 1609–1610.

Circle the letter that precedes the BEST answer to each of the following questions.

1. Which statement BEST expresses the main idea of this article?

    A. English merchants formed the Virginia Companies to share the costs of starting a colony in the Americas.

    B. Captain John Smith saved Jamestown when he took charge of the colony and bargained for supplies with the local Native Americans.

    C. Although the English established their first permanent settlement in the Americas in 1607, they had made attempts at settlement before this.

    D. In 1606 the London Company sent three ships—the *Discovery*, the *Susan Constant,* and the *Godspeed*—to start a colony in North America.

2. Read the following sentence from the passage.

    Raleigh hoped this group would form the nucleus of a farming community.

    What does the word *nucleus* mean as it is used here?

    A. center   B.   cell

    C. gathering   D.   portion

3. What happened to many of Jamestown's first settlers?

    A. They disappeared mysteriously.

    B. They learned how to live in the wilderness.

    C. They were infected with typhoid and malaria.

    D. They ran out of food and returned to England.

4. Which of the following ideas from the article is a FACT?

    A. Without a strong leader, Jamestown's future was in danger.

    B. Captain John Smith was a brave adventurer who became Jamestown's leader.

    C. Conditions in Jamestown improved somewhat under John Smith's leadership.

    D. Sir Walter Raleigh raised enough money to establish a colony in the Americas.

5. Why did John White leave the original colony at Roanoke in 1587?

   A. The settlers sent him to search for gold.

   B. He left to bring back more supplies and settlers.

   C. Queen Elizabeth wanted him to return to England.

   D. He wanted to visit his granddaughter, Virginia Dare.

6. What does the word *fortifications* mean as it is used in the second paragraph in the "John Smith Takes Charge" section?

   A. new rooms   B. front porches

   C. protective walls   D. unique designs

7. What is the author's main purpose in this article?

   A. to inspire   B. to inform

   C. to entertain   D. to persuade

8. If you wanted to make the point that life in America was difficult for the English settlers, which fact would be BEST to include in a research paper?

   A. In 1610 only sixty Jamestown settlers lived through the winter.

   B. In 1585 Raleigh sent a small group of men to Roanoke Island.

   C. In 1609 five hundred new settlers arrived in Jamestown from England.

   D. In 1587 John White led a second expedition to Roanoke but later returned to England.

9 When did White first go to Roanoke?

   A. in 1585

   B. in 1587

   C. in 1590

   D. in 1608

10. If the next subheading in this article were "New Leadership," which of the following subjects would most likely be covered in that paragraph?

   A. John Smith's plans for the future

   B. Sir Walter Raleigh's life in England

   C. the future of Jamestown after John Smith

   D. the future needs of the Virginia Companies

Read the following selection and answer the questions that follow.

The Three-Piece Suit

by Ali Deb—Translated by Alice Copple-Tošic´

1 This month, for the first time, the household budget has been met and . . . even left me a little supplement . . . I don't know why, I went against my habits and bought myself an elegant three-piece suit, tailored in a magnificent English fabric of lovely sky-blue—the color of sunlit days—in which the tailor's skill was displayed so well that one would say we were born together, one for the other. . . .

2 The buttons sparkling in the sun were like stars on the shoulder of a sailor swollen with courage. The spinning sensation that its price aroused did not last long, and I said to myself as I straightened my head and shoulders, "Tell me how you dress, and I'll say who you are."

3 I made my way without hesitation toward the largest café on the main street. As expected, my friends made a fuss over me, touching, feeling and dusting me with their fingers. I strutted, proud as a peacock. . . .

4 Naturally I paid for the drinks and left a fat tip for the waiter who gave me his best compliments. There was glib talk of the rise in prices and the high cost of living.

5 At this point one of them murmured into my ear, "What kind of shirt and tie are these?" Then he led me to a shop that was celebrated for the high quality of its merchandise and for its voraciousness. His good taste and affability were such that my pockets were emptied and it was only with great difficulty that I managed to pay the ticket home.

6 For one whole week, I concentrated on straightening out my accounts and forced myself to exactitude and strict austerity. I was thus obliged to forgo luxury and excess such as eggs and butter. I also reduced by half my consumption of meat and cigarettes and pretended to lack the time for entertainment with my friends. . . . I managed somehow or other to put my accounts back in order, while still not forgetting to trim my mustache, smooth my face with a close shave and spray myself with aftershave.

7 There I was, strolling about, puffed up with pride, on the main street, taking care to pass by the women since their tastes are more refined and assured and their eyes are sharper. . . . I heard as though a murmur in my ear, "The flaw is in your shoes." I turned and noticed a light blush on the face of a young girl. I counted the age of my shoes on my fingers. Goodness, how quickly the months had flown by. "Only a pair of shoes stands between me and perfection!" I chose a pair on Liberty Avenue, then returned to my friends. They directed their entire repertoire of flattering expressions my way and I was literally overcome by a delicious peace that was only troubled by the price of a cup of coffee. I almost proposed another spot in which to drink it but gave up; this café was better suited to my attire. My only recourse was a long but discreet sigh.

Copyright © Glencoe/McGraw-Hill, a division of The McGraw-Hill Companies, Inc.

Stop.

Standardized Test Practice   197

8   On the way home, the weather took a sudden turn and fine little drops fell on my oh-so-proud nose. "Abominable sky," and I bought an umbrella that saved me, in spite of its poor quality.

9   On Barcelona Square, I was accosted by young beggars. Their sullen faces, extended hands and supplications surrounded me to the point of suffocation. There were three of them, I handed fifty millimes to each one and, rid of their harassment, I gave a sigh of relief, but their leader came after me, repeating, "You're worth much more," showing the coin to all the passers-by. I bought his silence for double the amount. . . .

10   I walked prudently, taking the sidewalk, avoiding the dust on cars and jostling pedestrians. I fled the crowd and buses and never forgot to polish my shoes and iron my shirts carefully, often using the fire to dry them faster. The January cold suddenly came to mind and I anticipated the need to buy a coat and change my suit when winter had passed. Should I hold out my hand for a loan or draw directly from the company's cash box? Finally, I got on the train. I breathed in the fetid breath of the passengers. I leaned on the armrest of a seat; a lady grumbled and said to her neighbor, "They're even contesting our second-class seats." So I slipped into the first class where a seat and a supplementary fee of some consequence awaited me. I went into the local supermarket. It had been quite some time since I had taken care of my shopping. Upon seeing me, a neighbor literally shrieked for joy, shook my hand and then, raising his flat voice, asked me for a loan that I would have naturally refused him if I had not been wearing my suit.

11   I bought several items and held them in my arms against my chest. The salesgirl greeted me and unhooked a suitable basket. I had no other alternative but to deposit my purchases inside, and since the proper sort of people, my sort, buy without consideration for the price, I did not even bother to look at the cash register total. When I had returned home, my blood pressure was at its peak, my head was literally boiling, my tongue twisted and my chest heaving. I no longer saw where I walked or where I threw my jacket, vest, and trousers. I clenched my teeth and gritted them as I cursed the traps of this century and the folly of fools. I finally went back to being my old self and since that day no one has troubled me anymore.

Circle the letter that precedes the BEST answer to each of the following questions.

1. What does *austerity* mean?

   A. Practicing harsh self-discipline

   B. Living simply and plainly

   C. Following a strict diet

   D. Living unselfishly

2 In paragraph 10, to whom is the lady referring as "they" when she grumbles, "They're even contesting our second-class seats"?

   A. Beggars who are riding the train

   B. Men who are sitting in cars reserved for women

   C. Wealthy individuals who could afford better seats

   D. People who have taken money from their company's cash box

3 Which of the following phrases most clearly identifies one of the main conflicts in this story?

   A. Individual versus society

   B. Arabs versus Europeans

   C. Humans versus nature

   D. Males versus females

4. In paragraph 4, why did the narrator pay the check?

   A He remembered that it was his turn to pay.

   B. He was a generous man, so he usually bought beverages for others.

   C. He knew the custom that the last person to arrive should pay the check.

   D. He felt that the wealthiest person in the group should offer to pay for the beverages.

5. In paragraph 3, what does the alliterative phrase "proud as a peacock" do?

   A. Highlights the quick changes in the narrator's feelings

   B. Expresses the joy that the narrator feels about himself

   C. Emphasizes the seriousness of the narrator's purpose

   D. Shows the unhealthiness of the narrator's actions

6. Which action shows BEST the expected role of wealthy individuals in the culture in which the story is set?

   A. The narrator buys a coat for winter.

   B. The narrator loans money to a neighbor.

   C. The narrator buys a poor-quality umbrella.

   D. The narrator goes without eggs and butter for one week.

7. Which description BEST fits the personality of the narrator during most of the story?

   A. Careful though often tricked

   B. Assertive without being rude

   C. Intelligent but easily confused

   D. Proud yet eager to please others

8. What is the meaning of the term *voraciousness,* as it is used in paragraph 5?

   A. Ravenous hunger

   B. Excessive costliness

   C. Dignified stylishness

   D. Absolute truthfulness

9. What might be another appropriate title for this story?

   A. Birds of a Feather . . .

   B. A Stitch in Time . . .

   C. All That Glitters . . .

   D. A Penny Saved . . .

10. Which of the following BEST describes the narrator of the story?

   A. A poor student

   B. A wealthy investor

   C. A shop's proprietor

   D. An average employee

Word List

Word	Lesson	Word	Lesson	Word	Lesson
abduct	27	beset	4	disconsolate	19
abstinence	21	bibliophile	36	disparate	28
abyss	12	bland	16	dissident	24
accede	6	blazon	25	distill	10
accession	23	boorish	8	dividend	23
actuate	4	bowdlerize	5	doggerel	5
acuity	32	broach	34	dogma	14
adamant	12	brook	13	draconian	2
adduce	27	brusque	8	educe	27
adept	32	canon	20	elixir	13
adhere	34	capacious	17	ellipsis	28
aesthete	32	captious	9	elucidate	30
affluent	23	captivating	9	emancipate	9
alchemy	25	cerebral	34	embellish	23
allay	16	chauvinism	2	empirical	14
alleviate	4	chimerical	11	engaging	19
aloof	22	circumstantial	33	enigma	26
altruism	22	clandestine	11	entourage	13
amass	23	cognate	5	equanimity	18
ambivalence	36	collaboration	10	equilibrium	17
amoral	12	collusion	11	equity	23
analogy	30	combustion	16	equivalent	36
anarchy	12	commodious	17	erode	34
anemia	12	complementary	1	erudite	14
anesthetic	12	concatenation	35	ethnic	19
Anglophile	36	concession	6	evanescent	10
animosity	18	condiment	16	evangelize	20
animus	18	configuration	34	exemplify	1
annex	22	conifer	7	exorbitant	29
anthropoid	15	connoisseur	32	exotic	1
anthropomorphism	15	constituency	33	explicate	3
anticipatory	9	constrain	33	exploitation	22
apathetic	12	constrict	33	extenuation	21
aphorism	14	contemplative	14	extrapolate	25
apolitical	12	contend	19	fatalism	35
apotheosis	15	contrivance	35	felicitous	8
apparent	7	conundrum	26	fervent	4
appellation	5	convoluted	26	fester	4
apportion	29	corporeal	18	finesse	32
apt	28	corpulence	18	flawed	7
arbitrary	35	corpus	18	florescent	31
arid	31	corpuscle	18	formative	7
ascendancy	25	countervail	36	fortuitous	35
ascertain	34	cryptic	26	fractious	6
asset	23	curtail	29	fragmentary	6
assiduous	24	dearth	17	futile	25
assuage	16	deduce	27	gargantuan	17
astringent	33	defile	22	gastronomic	16
atheism	15	defray	6	grandiose	31
atrocity	19	deft	32	gravitate	10
atrophy	12	deluge	31	gullible	11
atypical	12	delusive	11	heartening	4
audacious	19	denizen	1	hector	2
augment	23	denude	16	humanitarian	4
auspices	3	desecrate	20	hybrid	10
auspicious	3	destitute	33	iconography	31
autocrat	13	devious	11	imperceptible	29
avail	36	dichotomy	1	impetuous	8
baleful	19	dire	4	implement	7
		discernible	29	implicate	3

Word	Lesson	Word	Lesson	Word	Lesson
imponderable	14	pedagogy	36	sedate	24
impunity	16	pedantic	36	sedative	24
incapacitate	9	pediatrics	36	sedentary	24
incendiary	7	perdition	20	sediment	24
inception	9	perpetual	13	seduce	27
incessant	19	perplex	26	serendipity	35
incipient	9	perspicacious	32	silhouette	2
incorporate	18	perspicuity	3	skepticism	14
ineffable	26	philanderer	36	smug	8
infidel	25	philanthropy	15	solidify	13
infinitesimal	29	pithy	28	soluble	26
infraction	6	plait	3	solvent	23
inimical	28	plausible	14	somber	10
inordinate	17	pliant	3	sparse	17
insidious	24	portent	21	specious	3
integral	28	pragmatic	1	speculate	3
inter	13	precedent	6	spontaneous	35
intercession	6	precocious	32	sporadic	31
introspective	3	predisposed	35	spurious	11
invest	1	premier	16	stature	33
irascible	8	pretentious	21	statute	33
labyrinth	26	prodigious	29	stentorian	2
lavish	29	profusion	10	strife	22
lingo	25	propagation	14	stringent	33
logistics	30	property	34	stylized	1
lucid	30	proselytize	20	sublime	31
lucre	23	protagonist	5	subsidiary	24
luminary	30	providential	35	sumptuous	13
Machiavellian	2	qualm	7	supersede	25
magnanimous	18	quandary	26	supine	8
maleficent	13	querulous	8	supplicate	20
manifest	28	rarefied	34	surreptitious	11
martinet	2	recede	6	susceptible	9
memoir	19	receptacle	9	sybarite	2
mendacity	11	recesses	34	tautology	30
mercurial	8	recuperate	9	tawdry	2
meritorious	28	refractory	6	tenable	21
meticulous	31	regalia	27	tenacious	21
mien	19	regime	27	tenant	21
misanthrope	15	regimen	27	tenuous	21
mobilize	4	regiment	27	tenure	21
modicum	29	regnant	27	terse	28
monologue	30	relucent	30	theocracy	15
monotheism	15	rendering	10	theological	15
muse	10	replica	1	therapeutic	16
nefarious	11	repudiate	14	translucent	30
neologism	30	residual	24	tribulation	7
numinous	26	restitution	33	truncate	31
opulence	17	retinue	21	tumult	22
ostensible	28	retrospect	22	unanimous	18
oxymoron	5	revel	22	unfounded	25
pantheon	15	rivulet	34	vagary	35
paradigm	5	rudimentary	25	vanguard	13
parameter	7	sacrilege	20	venerate	20
paramount	1	sardonic	8	vernacular	5
parity	29	satiate	17	vilification	22
parlance	5	saturnine	2	virtuoso	32
pastoral	5	savant	32	votary	20
patriarch	20	scintillate	10	wrought	31
paucity	17	séance	24	zealous	4